"This is the sort of book that sets big ideas and questions spinning in the reader's head and new ways of communicating the Gospel spiraling out of the preacher's soul."

—Leonard Sweet, best-selling author, professor, and chief contributor to sermons.com

"*Sermons Reimagined* is a good read! It offers creative approaches for anyone serious about connecting with a postmodern audience in search of direction. Based on a sound pulse of culture and trends just over the horizon, you'll find innovative ways to be God's interesting and relevant messenger. As one privileged to instruct future communicators of scriptural truth, this book is insightful and affirming!"

—Derek Voorhees, New Testament professor at Boise Bible College

"Rick blows up the past paradigm of preaching. In a creative expression he brings the sharing of God's Word into the 21st century. His understanding of the postmodern mind is enlightening. His approach is scholarly and fun. Rick has truly reimagined the sermon for the better!"

—Dr. Joseph C. Grana II, Dean of Pacific Christian College of Ministry & Biblical Studies

"If you have ever wondered how a semiotician writes a book on preaching, wonder no more! Rick Chromey models what he preaches. *Sermons Reimagined* offers hope and practical advice to those who refuse to believe that powerful preaching is a thing of the past. This book will help you discover afresh the power and wonder of beautiful feet (Romans 10:15)."

—Charles J. Conniry, Jr., Ph.D., Vice President and Dean of George Fox Evangelical Seminary and author of *Soaring in the Spirit: Rediscovering Mystery in the Christian Life*

Loveland, Colorado

Sermons REIMAGINED

PREACHING TO A FLUID CULTURE

RICK CHROMEY

SERMONS REIMAGINED:
PREACHING TO A FLUID CULTURE

Visit our website for more church leadership resources: **group.com**

Credits

Author: Rick Chromey

Editors: Amy Nappa and Bob D'Ambrosio

Assistant Editor: Kelsey Perry

Art Director: Amy Taylor

Cover Design: Kent Jensen

Interior Design: Andy Towler

Unless otherwise indicated, all Scripture quotations are taken from the *Holy Bible*, New International Version®, NIV® Copyright © 1973, 1978, 1984, 2011 by Biblica, Inc.® Used by permission. All rights reserved worldwide.

Library of Congress Cataloging-in-Publication Data

Chromey, Rick.
  Sermons reimagined : preaching to a fluid culture / by Rick Chromey. --
First American Paperback Edition.
       pages cm
  ISBN 978-1-4707-1670-7 (pbk. : alk. paper) 1. Preaching. I. Title.
  BV4211.3.C495 2014
  251--dc23
                                              2014032989

Printed in the United States of America

10 9 8 7 6 5 4 3 2 1   24 23 22 21 20 19 18 17 16 15

CONTENTS

Dedicated to

REBECCA AND RYAN

My two millennial, postmodern children.

Can you hear me now?

I love you.

ℭntroduction:
DEAF MEN DANCING

"We played the pipe for you, and you did not dance..."
—Jesus (Matthew 11:17)

We were born to boogie.

We were created to dance. Deep down in our bones we have an ancient, primitive beat. When we quiet our soul we hear its mystic rhythms. When we experience joy we are aware of its pounding pulse. In these moments of cadence, we sense God is real. We feel wholeness and worth. We connect and commune. We are secure and satisfied.

Unfortunately, such authentic moments are rare.

Most people, intentionally or not, pursue alternative forms of reality to feel the beat. We resolve the deep need to dance through Saturday night specials of self-medication, sexual exploration, and sensory experiences. We hop a joy ride only to crash and burn. We play with fire to heat our hunger but only scorch our soul with grief, anger, shame, guilt, doubt, and envy. We dance the night away only to wake up with a hangover addiction ruled by spiritual emptiness.

Our boogie shoes have holes in their soles.

It's Sunday morning in America.

Countless people (even more on Christmas and Easter) will gather in churches large and small, rural and urban, across the fruited plain. The faithful and faithless, pious and peeved, joyous and jaundiced, all come to connect, commune, and comprehend.

They arrive in various forms and fashions but consist primarily of three types.

The *regulars* attend faithfully to connect. They have friends in the house or a responsibility to fulfill. Church is a gathering space to serve, share, and submit.

The *fans* attend sporadically to commune. They want to experience God, but church is a hit or miss venture. Sleep, shopping, or sports are just as spiritually satisfying. Church is a consumer space to buy inspiration, purchase peace, or barter mercy.

The *seekers* are looking for God but rarely, if ever, go to church. Perhaps they've been hurt, even abused, by religion. Perhaps they're biblically and spiritually ignorant. Perhaps they're tired of religious people and the church. If they attend at all, it's nearly always due to a personal predicament that's bigger than their faith. Someone has died. They're emotionally distraught. They've been caught by addiction. Church is a crisis space.

Each group sits in the chairs with a different expectation.

- The regulars yearn for *insight*. It's a head issue.
- The fans want *inspiration*. It's a heart issue.
- The seekers hunger for *influence*. It's a life issue.

And most will go home largely disappointed. Deaf men (and women) walking.

It's why the American church is essentially on life support. Every year a thousand new churches will launch (most won't see their fifth birthday), while 4,000 will close. I'm not a math major, but that's a negative number: a big negative number.

Currently, America has around 350,000 congregations. Most of them are under 200 members, and many of them are dying on the vine. Meanwhile, outside the walls a world craves spirituality like a Saturday night buzz. They church hop for the best hope dealer and occasionally belly up to the bar, but they find no lasting intoxication in the spirits (especially the whine) of the church. Even the faithful are restless, particularly the Generation X and millennial generations (born after 1960).

What's this have to do with preaching?

To be honest, it has *everything* to do with preaching.

Thom and Joani Schultz wrote a challenging book titled *Why Nobody Wants to Go to Church Anymore*. It's an eye-opening title, but if we don't rethink some things, it'll prove prophetic. Currently, in some regions of America, less than 10 percent of people regularly attend church services. Even in the Bible Belt the worship waistline is shrinking.

In fact, if the title weren't stealing too much from my friends Thom and Joani, I would have named this book *Why Nobody Wants to Listen to Sermons Anymore*. I know that's a hard one to swallow because preachers have this delusional side that says the sheep hang on to every word they say. I used to have the same delusion (sometimes I still do). Preachers love to wax eloquent on the theological implications of substitutionary atonement, quote Luther and Lewis, sprinkle in Greek grammar, and season their sermons with hip video clips from 2005.

But they rarely observe their audience sleeping with eyes open. Disengaged. Distracted. Disappointed. Don't believe me? Just look around.

The music is playing, but the deaf aren't dancing. They have ears to hear, but the messages go in one side and out the other. That's why it's time to reimagine the sermon. Your sermon. My sermon.

Sure, the crowd will congratulate the preacher at the door and compliment his message. People are nice. They're grateful for the lecture but have heard it before, and it'll largely evaporate by mid-Sunday afternoon. Even worse, most won't care or put it into practice.

So here we are.

You. Me. And this book on preaching. In particular, a book on how to communicate to postmodern audiences, which is rapidly becoming the majority of people who still (or will) attend church.

I've preached for more than three decades and have taught pastoral ministry students how to teach (and preach) for most of that time. I've been a professional speaker for twenty-five years. And everything I learned, practiced, and believe about communication tattoos this book. In some ways I wrote this book as much for me as for you. But I'm dedicating it to my students. You know who you are.

I think I've got a few things figured out, particularly how postmodern culture receives and processes information (which is why few listen in church anymore), but I've got a lot of doubts too. I'm not sure I've got everything figured out and, frankly, that's a good thing. You never become more ignorant than the moment you profess to know it all. There's always something else to learn.

I do know that great preaching doesn't happen by accident, and, frankly, as a person in the pew I hear far too many fender benders, side swipes, and head-on collisions at 10 a.m. on Sunday morning. And I bet you have too. Like the Preacher from the Black Lagoon, a lot of Sunday sermons are hideous monsters sending people screaming to the exits. We can do better. We have to do better.

The deaf truly want to dance.

What I bring to the table is different. I'm a professional communicator. As mentioned, I make my living inspiring people with my words—in print and in person. People pay me to prick their thinking, shift their paradigm, or flame their passion. I've honed my unique style through countless hours of success and failure, years of studying master communicators, and taking intentional risks to discover fresh strategies for stale traditions.

Maybe that's why I sometimes feel like Isaiah.

My commission to pioneer and prophesy can produce complaint, criticism, and complacency. Isaiah was ordered by God to prophesy, or preach, to his people (Isaiah 6). His calling started with a "come to Jehovah" moment that crushed him to his core. He saw God in all his glory with his own eyes and promptly covered his lips. He was unclean, unworthy, unqualified. An angel appeared to tattoo his mouth, to purge the prophet's guilt and remove his sin. No more excuses, Isaiah.

Then God asks the million-dollar question: *"Whom shall I send?"* I've always found this question loaded with irony.

Isaiah was hanging out with God. He was clean, right, and loving life (and no doubt dancing a two-step). Then God throws a curveball. He needs some help and Isaiah is standing there with his hands raised to heaven in worship. The fact that God even has to ask the question is the irony. Isaiah is ready to go.

If we seek to communicate God's truth to a postmodern culture, we need to move from maintenance to mission, from passivity to proclamation, from a "woe is me" attitude to "go for me" gratitude. God wants to ruin our lives and in the process give us back our souls. He wants us to dance.

Isaiah was quick to answer: *"Here I am, send me!"*

He's like the kid in the back of class with the answer. He knows it and wants to share it. *Ooh-ooh-ooh! Pick me! I know! I know! I know!* The problem is he doesn't really *know.* Isaiah is quick to answer but soon learns going with God doesn't always equate to fame, fortune, or friends. Prophets are lonely people, and few profit in their times.

God then commissions Isaiah to preach to his people.

The good news is they'll listen. The bad news is they won't understand a word he'll say. The good news is they'll see his points. The bad news is they won't practice them. In fact, Isaiah has a rub: His preaching is going to make God's people grow calluses, hard hearts, and dull ears. These spiritually deaf are going to be clueless, ignorant, unappreciative, critical, and doubtful. They'll misunderstand, forget, snub, and snooze.

Sounds a bit like Sunday morning…but I digress.

Isaiah certainly wasn't expecting this. He asks, "For how long, Lord?" (Isaiah 6:11). This is just a test, right? It's just a trick to get their attention. It's a back door strategy to turn this ship around. How long?

God's reply brought no comfort.

"[I want you to preach] until the cities lie ruined and without inhabitant, until the houses are left deserted and the fields ruined and ravaged, until the Lord has sent everyone far away and the land is utterly forsaken. And though a tenth remains in the land, it will again be laid waste. But as the terebinth and oak leave stumps when they are cut down, so the holy seed will be the stump in the land" (Isaiah 6:11-13).

The good news? Buried within one of those stumps is a seed that'll change everything down the road…but you'll never experience it now.

So go…preach…and have a good time.

To his credit, Isaiah did preach that message to the deaf in his culture. He preached though no one got a clue. He prophesied though no one repented. He spoke though no one clapped, smiled, shook his hand, or patted his back. No one danced to his prophecies about a Messiah, seeded with hope and healing.

Some might argue Isaiah's poor results were due to his lousy speaking ability or poor communication strategies, but I respectfully disagree. I think Isaiah preached some good stuff and found creative ways to prophesy. The problem wasn't Isaiah; the problem was the people.

They were ignorant and insolent. They were bored and brazen. They were cold and calloused. A tough tone-deaf crowd for anyone, let alone a called prophet.

Fast forward to Sunday morning in America.

Untold numbers gather for a message from God. The circumstances of the week have calloused, hardened, bruised, nicked, and chilled them. The noise of culture leaves a ringing in their spiritual ears. Deaf men and women congregate.

The regulars come seeking insight but rarely receive depth. The preacher hasn't studied the passage deeply; he's only manipulated, converted, or expanded it. The regulars do their duty then leave feeling good but without any fresh insight. Most will forget everything by Wednesday.

The fans come because they favor the pastor's style or the worship band or both. They're simply seeking inspiration. *Make me feel good. I need a spiritual buzz.* But they won't attend church if the preacher hasn't heated his message for the heart. The academic homilies packed with big churchy words, theological rabbits, principles, and propositions only bore. The fans follow communicators. They leave feeling inspired and will be back in a few weeks for another fix.

The seekers come to fix a fret or heal a hurt. Church is a last resort option. They're in crisis and hunger for some influence, someone or something to get them through the mess. They don't mind some depth but it better make sense. They don't mind inspiration but find empty emotionalism manipulative and hypocritical.

On Sunday morning all three types gather to hear you preach the Gospel according to you.

- Will you have a message that's rich in insight? *The regulars hope so.*
- Will you have a message heated with inspiration? *The fans hope so.*
- Will you have a message primed to influence? *The seekers hope so.*

Master communicators have learned to speak to all three types. It is possible, but you have to rethink, reinvent, relearn, and reimagine. It's entirely feasible to tap the mind, prick the heart, and lead a life entirely in a single message.

It's possible to effectively speak to postmodern audiences, but you'll have to change because another Sunday monologue will fall flat. Our postmodern generations consume sound bites not sermons. They process information visually not verbally. They apply concepts through experiences and interaction, not passivity and lectures. Postmodern communicators employ stories to make The Story real.

MODERN PREACHING	POSTMODERN PREACHING
Preacher-Centered	Hearer-Centered
Points (Getting to the Point)	Process (Engaging the Process)
Content	Concepts
Monologue	Dialogue
Reason	Revelation
"Here I stand, I can do no other"	"I still haven't found what I'm looking for"
Focus: Right Thinking (Orthodoxy)	Focus: Right Behavior (Orthopraxis)
Organized: Never Changing	Organism: Ever Changing
Scripture Is a Textbook	Scripture Is a Letter
Creates Answers	Creates Questions

Jesus miraculously healed the deaf, but the truly hard of hearing were those with ears who resisted change. Tradition trumped truth. Ritual routed relevance. Personal style overwhelmed human need.

I don't know where the church will be in a hundred years (though I have my ideas). I am convinced the Sunday sermon as we know it today will not be there. The sermon, as known today, is the by-product of modernity. The Reformation elevated Scripture and sermon while the Enlightenment boxed both formats within argument and mechanics. The sermon became central to modern worship (replacing the Eucharist, or Lord's Supper, as the point of gathering—a 1,500 year tradition!). With the rise of rhetoric came propositional preaching, or preaching with points. Preachers pontificated, debated, proposed, and pounded their pulpits.

For five centuries this frame worked because modern culture processed information verbally, mechanically, and through centralized voices: politician, professor, and preacher. The emergence of television shifted these voices to screens. Televised political debates. Public television. Televangelism.

But the recent technological shift—powered not just by television but the Internet and cellphones—has completely changed the game. Information has been decentralized. Authority has been flattened. Every person is a content producer, preacher, professor, and politician thanks to Web and wireless media. Those born since 1960 have experienced and embraced the shift more than older generations, but with every new generation the age of modernity fades.

At the heart of this book is a radical commitment to communication.

If we don't learn to communicate with postmodern culture, the death of the modern church—including the sermon—will be hastened. No church is immune. Reinvent or die. There is no plan B.

But I also believe, to those who master how to spiritually speak into a postmodern context, the brightest days of the church lay ahead. Postmodern preaching will reimagine the church as relevant and real. What will that look like? Well, that's what the following pages are all about.

Another prophet named Ezekiel was called to prophesy to dead bones.

We are commissioned to preach to people deadened by religion and spiritually dry.

Ezekiel spoke, and the dry bones resurrected to form a massive human army.

Similarly, we are called to communicate in a manner that causes dry bones to rise and deaf men to dance. Our messages focus upon a Messiah who fixes the messes. Postmoderns love Jesus. They just don't understand, respect, appreciate, or like the lecture. The deaf and dry hunger to be human, and incarnational Christianity (where God became human as Jesus) sings louder than any other religious idea, holy philosophy, or spiritual ideology.

Postmodern preaching calls deaf men to dance.

So get your boogie shoes on—it's time to tango!

It's time to reimagine the sermon.

Chapter One:
WHAT JUST HAPPENED?

> "When evening comes, you say, 'It will be fair weather, for the sky is red,' and in the morning, 'Today it will be stormy, for the sky is red and overcast.' You know how to interpret the appearance of the sky, but you cannot interpret the signs of the times."
>
> —Jesus (Matthew 16:2-3)

Change is a beautiful thing.

Just ask a butterfly. Or the owner of a new car. Or an infant with a dirty diaper. Jimmy Buffet was right: Changes in latitudes spark changes in attitudes. New Year's Eve is a global cultural celebration. Though nothing truly changes when the clock strikes midnight (except the year's number), we still kiss loved ones, pop champagne corks, and watch various objects drop like there's no tomorrow. The old is gone. The new is here.

Deep down we all hunger for change, yet we also know there's a price for transformation.

From the day we're conceived, humans are constantly changing. We change physically, emotionally, cognitively, and spiritually. We change communities, contexts, and cultures. We change clothes and careers, hobbies and habits, direction and duties. We change beliefs and biases, presuppositions and promises, rules and reasons. As we grow older the changes become painfully clear. We lose our hair, gray, wrinkle, and slow down. We change our marital status, family dynamic, and financial situation. We change our hearts, minds, and bodies through self-improvement strategies. Change happens every day, even every moment.

Change also hurts. It's rooted in pain, discomfort, or wounds—past or present (with a healthy amount of fear about the future). Change is hard. We have to work to lose the pounds, quit the habit, or pay the debt. Change forces new chapters. We learn (often the hard way) to rehabituate to fresh circumstances, context, or culture. And, let's be brutally honest, change rarely happens without frustration, fear, and failure. We all hunger to become butterflies but find the metamorphosis cocooned in crisis and conflict. It's also difficult to spread our wings and fly if all we've ever done is crawl and creep. Change is particularly painful if we didn't ask for it, want it, or pursue it.

Just Do It!

Want to *feel* change? Fold your hands. Now switch your hands so the OPPOSITE thumb is on top and hold it for several minutes. How does it feel? Go ahead and admit it. It feels wrong. It's not what you're used to. But give it time and it's not so bad.

This book is all about change. In particular, the need to change our communication style if we want to be heard by postmodern generations. Trust me, the process will feel uncomfortable, strange, and even wrong at times. We relish our comfort zones, but if we resist change in a changing world we'll also lose influence. We'll lose the ability to connect and communicate. The message is eternal but the methods (and messenger) are not…just ask Kodak.[1]

Or the Apostle Paul:

> To those not having the law **I became like one** not having the law (though I am not free from God's law but am under Christ's law), so as to win those not having the law. To the weak **I became weak,** to win the weak. **I have become all things** to all people so that **by all possible means** I might save some. I do all this for the sake of the gospel, that I may share in its blessings. (1 Corinthians 9:21-23)

In this Corinthian passage, Paul outlines Communication 101. *Know your audience. Contextualize your message. Creatively communicate it.* And that's the problem I see with most preaching today including my own: it's self-serving. I listen to a lot of preachers and hear hundreds

Digital Killed The Photo Star

In 1975 a Kodak engineer actually invented the first digital camera. But when he presented the idea to his company about a "filmless camera," they shut it down. Kodak was the number one photography company in the world but failed to embrace an emerging digital economy in the 1990s. By 2012, Kodak was bankrupt.

of sermons every year. Many of them exegete the Greek, investigate ancient Greco-Roman-Judeo culture, analyze literary nuances, and create insightful central theses. (Whew!) Most preachers, trained in biblical interpretation (hermeneutics) and preaching (homiletics), have not studied educational theory and practices. Consequently, they know stuff (good stuff), but they don't know how to creatively communicate the stuff.

When I ask preachers to consider techniques that are more experiential and interactive, I hear a lot of excuses, rationales, and alibis.

The number one response? It's not "my style."

Ah, but that's the problem. Preaching isn't about me and what I like. We preach so that people might hear, believe, and become like Jesus (Romans 10:13-15). What I prefer and how I want to preach is actually immaterial. My style can change. My methods *should* change. And the reason I change is so *they* can hear.

Now let me be clear and honest: If the majority of your congregation is gray-haired, blue-haired, or no-haired, this book isn't for you. You're preaching to the geriatric choir, and they're grooved toward a communication style truly old school (lecture). That's okay. And while I hope you'll keep reading, I understand if you don't. But if you speak primarily to under-55 types or you're ready to draw younger generations to your message, then keep reading. This book is for you…or really for them.

The journey of a thousand miles begins with a single step and no small amount of retrospect. We can't go forward without looking back; to exegete the future, we must start by plumbing the past. In the past fifty years everything has changed. The younger generations born since 1960 feel it the most, especially at church. They feel like they're spiritually folding their hands different every time they enter a Sunday service. Awkward. Uncomfortable. Even wrong.

In the movie *The Matrix*, the character named Neo is challenged with an ultimatum:

> *This is your last chance. After this, there is no turning back.*

> *You take the blue pill—the story ends, you wake up in your bed and believe whatever you want to believe. You take the red pill—you stay in Wonderland and I show you how deep the rabbit-hole goes.*[2]

If you want to communicate to postmodern generations, it's time to swallow the red pill and learn what just happened. But beware: This rabbit hole runs deep.

CHANGE HAPPENS

In the sciences of paleontology and geology there's a rule: "*The key to the past is the present.*" In other words, observation of what is (a fossil) can help scientists piece together what happened (an ancient event). For futurists, the rule changes slightly: "*The key to the future is the past.*" In my doctoral studies, I learned semiotics (how to read cultural signs). Lesson one: You can't chart the future without parsing the past. It's nothing new. Weathermen do it every day. Every weather prediction relies upon what's happened in the past. Yesterday's weather patterns forge tomorrow's forecasts. Anomalies occasionally happen but, overall, Solomon was right: There's nothing new under the sun.

Jesus criticized the religious leaders of his day for their inability to "interpret the signs of the times" (Matthew 16:3). It's no different today. Cultural relevance isn't a sin, but we also mustn't confuse fads with shifts. Fads fade. Shifts reinvent.

Therefore, in order to grasp the postmodern shift and reveal fresh strategies for communication to the postmodern mind, we must first gaze into the rearview mirror of history. We need to push rewind and review what happened then search for cultural clues from the past. History will prove insightful for where we're going.

THE MODERN MACHINE

Modernity is a loosely and classically framed period from 1500 to 2000. During these five centuries, civilized cultures experienced renaissance and reformation, periods of enlightenment, sprinkled with scientific and industrial revolutions. But modernity didn't just happen. It was a cultural reaction to major technological innovations that emerged between the 14th and 16th centuries. These "mega-techs" shifted society and spawned new cultural languages (how society processes and communicates information).

Such "mega-techs" aren't new. In fact, about every 500 years there are seismic technological innovations that charge and change civilized cultures, whether it's an innovation in communication (paper, printing), war (crossbow, gun powder), industry (furnace, watermill), or transportation (arch bridge, compass).

Technology That Changed How Cultures Operated/Interacted

700-300 B.C.	200 B.C.–A.D. 200	A.D. 300-700	A.D. 800-1200
Crane	Paper	Paddlewheel Boat	Gunpowder
Crossbow	Watermill	Horse Collar	Movable Type
Blast Furnace	Arch Bridge	Greek Fire (weapon)	Mariner's Compass

It's important to remember most technology until the Middle Ages was confined to local culturals and ethnic contexts. Even larger empires like Greece and Rome were largely landlocked to Europe, the Middle East, and North Africa. During the Renaissance, civilized cultures began to explore new worlds and, in occupying these territories, inculcated their culture within fresh contexts. Ships sailed virgin oceans and discovered new products, beasts, and lands.

Modernity, unlike previous shifts, proved more global. The world got smaller, especially as later technological advances in transportation (ships, planes, automobiles) allowed man to travel farther at faster speeds. Wherever civilized cultures dwelled, modern technology ruled. And three "mega-techs," in particular, shifted and changed the cultural languages of modernity:

- The **printing press** (Johannes Gutenberg, 1450)
- The **mechanized clock** (circa 1400)[3]
- The **telescope** (Hans Lippershey and Zacharias Janssen, 1608)

The Renaissance (1300-1600), which literally means "rebirth," reimagined the world and introduced new ideas to western culture. Of course, the ability to mass produce information through print technology was most significant. In fact, the printing press is without question the greatest invention of the last millennium for its influence upon all cultural institutions.

For example, the European university had been around since the 11th century, but the emergence of mass media (books) spawned spectacular growth in academic institutions. Europe boasted 29 universities just four centuries after the University of Bologna opened in 1088, but between 1400 and 1800, that number exploded to 143! The Renaissance birthed the Enlightenment, or the Age of Reason. Rene Descartes (1596-1650), the father of modern philosophy, famously quipped, "I think, therefore I am." His words continue to control Western and modern thinking to this very day.

The printed page ruled modernity through various formats: books, periodicals, journals, telegraphs, bulletins, letters, photographs, handbills, posters, and postcards. Words were recorded and catalogued. The first book Gutenberg printed was the Holy Scriptures, or *hagios biblos* (Holy Book). Later, Robert Stephanus parsed the Bible into verses during the mid-16th century. In some church circles, the moniker "people of the Book" was promoted to announce their "biblical" Christianity. The problem? This tag is technological not theological.

In a modern word-based culture, communication shifted from short homilies into lengthier speeches, sermons, lectures, and monologues. Modern speakers (and preachers) relied upon logic, rhetoric, debate, illustration, quotes, analogy, and outline to secure their points to the modern mind. In the 20th century, radio and television spawned the age of the communicator. The lectern, pulpit, and microphone emerged as symbols of authority, popularity, and eventually celebrity.

The mechanized clock impacted culture as much as the printing press. It forged a new frame of reference and reinvented time into "chunks." Time was boxed within seconds, minutes, and hours. A clock "told" time and that time was authoritative. The mechanization of time invoked its own philosophical, theological, and psychological consequences. Modernity ran like clockwork. Truth was packaged and objectified first into arguments, then behind walls, and, in the church world, eventually closeted within denominations. If your truth wasn't my truth then you were wrong, even heretical.

Modern institutions mechanized and operated by the clock. Factories, schools, and churches employed assembly-line, industrial models to manufacture widgets, students, and disciples. In modern Christianity, church services were eventually framed to fit inside 60 to 75 minutes, with multiple "inside the box" worship gatherings. Theology was also systemized. The clock controlled spirituality and packaged faith within principles, programs, and curriculum. The preacher controlled the service like a master of ceremonies.

The third modern mega-tech was the telescope. This innovation was culturally significant, for it elevated man as the superior center of the universe. Isaac Newton proposed a closed universe that resembled one big box. Newtonian physics influenced science for centuries and defined all of life within time and space. Philosophically, this centralizing of authority gave rise to humanism (Erasmus, Machiavelli), empiricism (Locke, Bacon), rationalism (Descartes, Spinoza), and skepticism (Hume, Voltaire). In a sense, Darwinism is a scientific and philosophical argument for man's ultimate centrality and superiority. He's king of the universe.

As a result of the influence of the printing press, mechanized clock, and telescope, fresh cultural languages emerged. If you listen, you can still hear them speak.

Word-based. Mechanism. Passive. Closed.

For centuries modern culture reflected boxes within a box (confined by time and space), operated mechanically, and interacted through word-based communication. In fact, most churches still reflect modern sensibilities.

Christianity is confined within walls and by times, or "order of service." Churches operate like businesses with very select hours, opening one to two hours a week inside spiritual boxes known as "sanctuaries" or "worship centers." These sacred spaces are logically arranged into rows, where the chairs and pews are often bolted to the floor or connected to each other. Church is locked within time and space. It's even in our vocabulary when we say, "I'm going to church" or "I went to church."

The modern church DNA revealed a passive flock led by centralized authority (preacher, priest) in a baptism of words (song and sermon, liturgy and lesson). The church of modernity was a closed spiritual universe that proudly flew (and still flies) its theological banners to label her boxes (Catholic, Lutheran, Episcopal, Presbyterian, Methodist, Baptist, Nazarene, Pentecostal, and countless other "non-denominational" denominations). It's no wonder we struggle to grow disciples. The

DNA of "sit and soak" rarely becomes seek and serve, except to the few who are called into specialized Christian vocations.

For centuries, centralized authorities allowed the powerful, rich, and educated to create social frames and control media. In a modern world it was possible to censor information. Leadership was centralized around the educated: preachers, vicars, presidents, chiefs, generals, bosses, professors, and principals. The rise of the educated elite reinforced the pulpit (sermon) and lectern (lecture) as a power tool. The one who controlled the church and school ruled society. This is why most Protestant churches today still exhaust more than 50 percent of their worship time with the sermon.

In a word, modernity was about *control*.

Modern theology, science, and philosophy reflected a controlled universe. Machines were controlled objects. Unlike an agricultural society that depends on the blessing of nature (sun, rain, dirt), the factory belched a 9 to 5 job to create a new economic class known as "the middle." Middles ruled in modernity. The bell curve. Suburbs. Middle management. Mainstream media. Middle of the road. In a machine culture, everyone was the same (a product)…except the educated elite. Knowledge was power and prominence.

In the spring of 1912, a British ocean liner with a titanic moniker sailed her maiden voyage from Southampton, England to New York City. On board were 2,224 passengers, divided into three classes: first, second, and third (or "steerage"). The wealthy elite boasted millionaires like John Jacob Astor IV and Margaret "Molly" Brown. The affluent enjoyed the best in opulent comfort, five-star dining, and luxurious entertainment, including ornate cabins, a gymnasium, swimming pool, and libraries. The steerage passengers, mostly European emigrants, lived in small, shared cabins with few bathrooms and little food. Sandwiched between the two were second-class passengers who experienced better comforts than steerage but clearly not as pampered as first class.

The Titanic boasted the best in machinery, navigation, and communication. The ship, by design, was unsinkable and the fastest of the seafaring fleets. The captain of the ship controlled the experience while everyone, including the crew, lived in little boxes segregated by their wealth. Any mixing of the classes was unintentional and momentary.

Around midnight on April 14, the unthinkable happened: The Titanic struck an iceberg and started to sink. Within a couple hours, the mighty ship slipped beneath the icy 28-degree dark waters and death came quickly. The lifeboats deployed serviced the wealthy, particularly women and children. By dawn, more than 1,500 passengers were dead while only 710 were rescued.

The Titanic is a potent parable for the demise of modernity and, in many ways, is a historical marker signaling the beginning of the end. Within three decades, two world wars, the Great Depression, and a growing global cultural awareness (helped by new emerging technologies) would prove to be icebergs that sunk modernity.

Moderns engineered environments that reflected the superiority of man's knowledge and capacity for control. Therefore, creative thought was considered "thinking outside the box." Social institutions were framed inside acceptable boxes. Modern cities were laid out in squares, spreading from the center. The rich lived in their box (usually on a hill), while the social steerage dwelt in slums (at the bottoms). Later the post-war suburbs created a segregated middle class, sandwiched between the rural farmer and the inner city factory worker, who commuted in moving boxes called cars.

In a modern culture the church thrived. The exclusivity of Christianity proved successful in a world of boxes. A church operated both as its own universe and university. In fact, many European modern churches had box seats. Each family worshipped within a high-walled box, uniquely decorated to their taste. This is why pulpits were positioned high. Inside the box, worshippers had to look up and listen to the sermon. The preacher was in full control. Eventually the walls were gone but the pews remained, revealing row after row of passivity.

Church resembled a library, a place of sacred silence around two books: the Bible and hymnal. Church services were secularized, particularly in the 1970s, to reflect a performance-based "Woodstock" worship frame. Today's contemporary worship (and preaching) now resembles a concert with a spiritual lecture.

It's no wonder fewer and fewer people are listening anymore.

And it explains why fewer and fewer of the emerging generations even "go to church." Church is a place for getting married and buried and part of Christmas and Easter traditions. If you think about it, people rarely attend church to hear the message anyway. They go to see family and friends and to experience God. A smaller percentage will go to serve, give offerings, and to hear a biblical message. It's not that people dislike sermons. It's just not as significant as preachers think.

Here's a test: If you shaved off five minutes of your message every week and used the extra time for testimony, worship experiences, creative prayer, and music, would anyone care? Or even notice?

Modernity created a box—church. But postmoderns live beyond boxes.

In the 20th century, the emergence of television technology changed the cultural language from WORD to VISUAL. Emerging generations now process information visually or, better, multi-visually. Just like the printing press, mechanized clock, and telescope ushered in modernity (and released culture from 500 years of ignorance during the Dark Ages), television has reinvented communication.

Two other mega-techs—the cellphone and the Internet—have contributed to the emergence of a postmodern world.

What are the new postmodern cultural languages?

Interactive. Open. Experiential. Image-driven.

The signs of the times are clear. Everything has changed. The postmodern generations no longer relate to modern strategies. And that's why we need to think different.

Endnotes

1. For an excellent treatment of Kodak's demise, read Thom Schultz's blog titled "The Church's Frightful Kodak Moment," http://holysoup.com/2014/01/15/the-churchs-frightful-kodak-moment/.

2. International Movie Database (IMDB), *The Matrix*, "Quotes," http://www.imdb.com/title/tt0133093/trivia?tab=qt&ref_=tt_trv_qu.

3. Identifying the exact date for mechanical clocks is very difficult, given there were mechanisms for hourly clocks that emerged in the 1200s. The detailed "spring-driven" mechanization of the clock, indicating minutes and seconds, happened in the late 15th and 16th centuries. Early mechanical clocks were woefully inaccurate and inadequate timekeepers.

Chapter Two:
NEW WINESKINS

"He told them this parable: 'No one tears a piece out of a new garment to patch an old one. Otherwise, they will have torn the new garment, and the patch from the new will not match the old. And no one pours new wine into old wineskins. Otherwise, the new wine will burst the skins; the wine will run out and the wineskins will be ruined. No, new wine must be poured into new wineskins.'"

—Jesus (Luke 5:36-38)

The silver disc is dead.

It's the technology formerly known as the CD or DVD.

Don't believe me? Just try to sell one to your local pawnshop (who's in the business of flipping stuff for a buck). When a pawnbroker won't buy, it's the beginning of the end. You know what that means, don't you? That wonderful DVD (or Blu-Ray) collection will soon be obsolete along with the CD/DVD player. Digital killed the silver disc star.

Need another example? How about that old 1990s box television? You know, the monster square hunk of plastic and glass trapped in a world that's gone flat-screen (or will it be "curved"?). You can't give those beasts away at yard sales, and thrift stores no longer waste shelf space with them. All across America garages are littered with these obsolete televisions.

Obsolete technology is everywhere. Typewriters. Cassettes. 8-tracks. Rotary phones. Polaroid cameras. PalmPilots. Mimeographs. Black and white televisions. Floppy discs. Flannelgraphs. Overhead, slide, and film projectors. Answering machines. Carburetors in cars. Calculator watches. Pay phones. Can you hear me now? *Good.*

But more change is in the wind.

Technologies marked for obsolescence include the mouse, desktop and laptop computers, photocopiers, printers, newspapers, books, landline phones, satellite and cable television, Redbox, checkbooks, credit and debit cards, and car, hotel, and house keys. That's why we can't get too comfortable in our communication strategies. Change is happening faster than ever. You've heard carpe diem, or "seize the day," but even that's impossible in a world spinning at the speed of life. The best you can do is position yourself to seize tomorrow, for by the time you've got today handled, it's gone and you're left wondering, "What just happened?"

Technology certainly changes how we interact and learn and how we're entertained and influenced. Five hundred years ago the advent of print technology reinvented communication, putting the scroll and pen out of business. A printing press could mass-produce information. Today the click of a mouse does the same thing.

In the early hours of December 7, 1941, the U.S. territory of Hawaii was attacked by Japan. News of the bombing on Pearl Harbor back in the mainland proved slow, mostly by radio, interrupting Sunday afternoon programming. Sunday night special edition newspapers rushed out coverage, but most of America didn't read anything exhaustive on the attack until the morning paper on December 8. Newsreels of the attack wouldn't be shown for several months. Even President Roosevelt didn't address the nation (by radio) until a full day after the attack.

In 1941, all news was centralized and controlled, even censored, by the major media outlets. Editors determined what made front page or got buried on page 15.

Fast forward to breaking news today. Depending on our desire for connection, news comes to us 24/7/365. Our smartphones, computers, and televisions now inform us (I'm live-streaming my noon-day television news as I write this sentence). News now finds us. We can even choose our own news bias (Fox or MSNBC, The Huffington Post or Drudge Report). Satellite boasts dozens of news-oriented channels, from CNN to C-SPAN and Fox Business to the Weather Channel. Online there are countless news outlets, constantly updating and breaking news. And then there's Twitter, YouTube, Facebook, and other social networks. When news breaks, it instantly goes global.

Everything has changed. And like Jesus said, if we don't change the wineskins they'll be a bust. In a sound bite culture you can't keep

Generation "Unchristian"

In 2007, David Kinnaman and Gabe Lyons argued from their extensive studies how nearly 4 in 10 American Generation Xers (37 percent) and millennials (40 percent) were "outsiders to Christianity." In comparison, only 27 percent of Boomers and 23 percent of elder generations were "outsiders."

Even more troubling is their overall impression of Christianity, which continues to worsen. In 2007, less than 1 in 5 had a good impression of Christianity. Ironically, many of these Gen Xers and millennials also grew up in our children and youth ministries. What went wrong?[1]

preaching like it's 1941. Similar to the compact disc, lengthy lectures are a dying format. It doesn't matter if you're preaching on Sunday morning or teaching on Tuesday night. It doesn't even matter if you're the president of the United States delivering the State of the Union.[2] The only ones tuned in by choice are older, grayer, and balder.

Albert Einstein is attributed as saying insanity is doing the same thing over and over again yet expecting different results. By that definition, Sunday morning is clearly America's most insane time of the week, because the church as we know it is broken and we just keep doing the same things over and over.

Generation X left the church in the 1980s and 1990s. The millennials exited in the 2000s and continue to remain AWOL. Countless studies have confirmed the postmodern generations, born since 1960, aren't leaving Christianity, but they are leaving the *modern* church. They are leaving the old wineskin. They find it irrelevant and boring, and they're busting out.

Generation "Religiously Unaffiliated"

A 2012 Millennials Survey Report by the Public Religion Research Institute revealed a disturbing rise in the "religiously unaffiliated" among the millennial generation. As children, only 11 percent claimed that moniker but by college age 1 in 4 were in this group (a 14 percent increase).

Furthermore, 8 in 10 religiously unaffiliated millennials view contemporary Christianity as "judgmental" (84 percent) and "hypocritical" (84 percent). And only 18 percent of the religiously unaffiliated view present-day Christianity as relevant to their lives.[3]

According to church researcher Dr. Scott Thumma of Hartford University, between 2007 and 2012, the "unaffiliated" category of churchgoers increased between 3 and 4 percent. Postmodern generations show the greatest disconnect: Generation X (21 percent) and millennials (30-34 percent).[4] A 2012 Pew Research study confirmed the millennial generation is rapidly "losing faith" in God and doubting God's existence (down 15 percent in 5 years).[5]

And yet, there is a silver lining. Younger generations who remain faithful to Christianity are choosing reinvention over renovation. In their book *The Outsider Interviews*, Jim Henderson, Todd Hunter, and Craig Spinks argue:

> Not only is there a divide between insiders and outsiders, but there is a divide between insiders and insiders. Thousands of young Christians are staying under the big ten of Christianity but refusing to toe the party line... this pragmatic, postmodern bunch is staying home and fighting for a new kind of Christianity.[6]

A new kind of Christianity demands new wineskins. Unfortunately, the modern (Protestant) church seems hopelessly bottled in a tradition it can't escape or willingly leave to history. Instead we just repaint, repair, and resize old wineskins. It's insanity by definition.

For example, in recent years the solution to reach postmodern generations has been to reinvent the worship experience. So we moved from piano and organs to guitars and drums. We transitioned from hymns to praise. We ditched the hymnal for visual presentations. And while these paint jobs certainly help, most contemporary churches still gripped tightly the wineskin of one-way communication. The sermon in the Protestant church remains center stage. Worship is performed by only a few. Everyone else just watches.

I think it's time for a new wineskin.

The postmodern generations, born since 1960, are different. They think differently. They process information differently. They worship differently. They respond to God's Word differently.

It's easy to see why if we just rewind the clock.

REWIND: 1964

When Bob Dylan penned his prophetic 1964 folk song to the changing times, no one imagined what the next fifty years would bring or how right Dylan would prove. Besides the *Jetsons*, a futurized cartoon set in the year 2062, and Gene Roddenberry's *Star Trek* (which he dreamed up in 1964), most of America still happily inhabited the 1950s cultural motif (and some might argue the 1850s). And then three national events in 1963 and 1964 rearranged everything and everyone. It was the societal earthquake heard around the world.

It began with a dream in the late summer of 1963 when Martin Luther King, Jr. and a quarter million people of all races marched on D.C. for black civil rights. Less than three months later another visionary, President John F. Kennedy, was gunned down in Dallas, silencing Camelot.[8] A grief-stricken American populace gathered around a box in their living rooms for collective national mourning. Television changed America that day and instantaneously fashioned a new window to the world. News now lived. You could see it. And it was now in color. In 1964 only 3.1 percent of U.S. households owned a color television, but by 1974 nearly 7 in 10 homes watched color programming.[9]

Then those television sets were rocked (and rolled) in February 1964 when the Beatles landed in America. The Fab Four reinvented modern music and culture in the 1960s. Between 1963 and 1964, the last Studebaker was produced while the Ford Mustang debuted. BASIC computer code was introduced, the foundational language of the computer age. Sony unveiled the first home videocassette recorder that now allowed consumers to time-shift television programming. The cassette tape was created for recording and playing audio. AT&T released touch-tone phones. The U.S. Postal Service started using zip codes.

King. Kennedy. Beatles.

It was a seismic string of cultural events.

From the mid-1960s to the late 1990s, the modern world was now on a death march. With each succeeding technological innovation, emerging generations (Gen X, Millennial, iTech) began to process information through visual, digital, and experiential formats.

BOOMER (1943-1960)	GENERATION X (1961-1981)	MILLENNIAL (1982-2004)	iTECH (2005-present)
Black & White TV	Color TV	Plasma TV	HD and 3D TV
Rabbit Ears	Cable	Satellite	Streamed
n/a	Pong/Donkey Kong	Super Mario/Sim City	Angry Birds/TBD
Vinyl Record	Cassette	CD	MP3
Rotary Phone	Touch-Tone Phone	Cellphone	Smartphone
Postal Mail	Postal Mail	Email	Text

If you're over 55, you grew up in a black and white, analog, word-based America. But your children, grandchildren, and great grandchildren grew up and are growing up in a color, digital, visual world.

That's why if you're still driving a Studebaker and preaching like it's 1960, you're as obsolete as a Polaroid camera, 8-track cassette, and Betamax. In fact, if 1963 and 1964 was the cultural earthquake, then 2000 and 2001 was the unheralded rise of this brand-new world. Since that time our previously modern world rehabituated as a digital, global, multi-visual, experiential, interactive, postmodern culture. It looks nothing like 1960. It took nearly four decades for the old world to sink, but it's now largely gone, like the Titanic, into the deep recesses of history. Change happens and sometimes it changes everything and everyone. Dylan's song is history. Consider the times now changed.

Jesus' first miracle transformed water into wine (John 2:1-11). Evidently the festive punch was gone and this social faux paux put the wedding party in a serious pickle. Because first-century tradition demanded a weeklong party with abundant drink, the unexpected depletion of wedding wine was a tragedy. Normally, the more expensive, fine wine was served early, while watered-down versions were passed around later in the week.

New Is Always New

Did you know that "new" appears 280 times in Scripture? God is always wanting to do something new.

"Therefore, if anyone is in Christ, the **new creation** has come: The old has gone, the **new** is here!" (2 Corinthians 5:17).

"Because of the Lord's great love we are not consumed, for his compassions never fail. They are **new every morning**; great is your faithfulness" (Lamentations 3:22-23).

"See, I am doing a **new thing**! Now it springs up; do you not perceive it? I am making a way in the wilderness and streams in the wasteland" (Isaiah 43:19).

"Praise the Lord. Sing to the Lord a **new song**, his praise in the assembly of his faithful people" (Psalm 149:1).

The fact that Jesus creates a new wine isn't surprising, but rather his refusal to use a traditional wineskin at all. Instead, Jesus instantly brewed 120 gallons of Grade A Divine wine and bottled his signature swill inside jars reserved for ceremonial washing. That's right, he used water with which people washed their hands. He basically changed washroom water into fine wine. Now that's a miracle!

It's a good message for the church. If our wine (message) is stale or stuck, if our Sunday morning worship looks more like a funeral than a wedding, then maybe it's time we let Jesus work a miracle. But we also need to imagine fresh wineskins for the innovative spirits God is brewing. Jesus-wine is utterly divine and overflows with grace, relevance, and beauty. If you try to pour it into an old wineskin, the vase will fissure, crack, and explode. New wineskins are flexible and moldable. They bend and build to hold the new wine so it can ferment with flavor. New wineskins aren't trapped by tradition but are ready for relevance. They aren't containers for conservation but vessels for vision. Wineskins are temporary, constantly changing, and always new.

The modern church wineskin is cracking. Face it, the sermon leaks and has lost its flavor. Postmodern generations desperately seek to savor Jesus-wine, but find churchianity unattractive, boring, and irrelevant. In fact, I wonder if God (who relishes new things) doesn't look down at our Sunday messages and yawn, "Really? I've heard that one before."

THE END IS NEW

Since 2000, the majority of civilized culture interacts as a cyber digital world. Google is the new professor. YouTube is the new media. Facebook is the new mall. Twitter is the new bumper sticker. Wikipedia is the new library.

Digital media killed the photograph, the CD, and now the DVD (and very likely the book). Communication is 24/7/365. People interact continuously and everywhere they have access. The products we buy are personalized. One size no longer fits all. You can travel the world and never leave your home.

A postmodern culture is rich in irony and oxymorons.

Things get bigger, while they also get smaller. Things get faster, while they also get slower. The more we futurize, the more we embrace ancient tradition. The more we advance in science, the more we hunger for spirituality. Dr. Leonard Sweet tags this as the "double ring" of postmodern culture and encourages EPIC (experiential, participatory, image-based, and connective) strategies to reach emerging postmodern generations.[10]

Television (and later visual technologies from gaming to GPS) has transitioned us from a word to image culture. Younger generations process information multi-visually; that is, they can ingest multiple moving images simultaneously. Watch any network or cable news channel. The talking head remains, but plenty of action and movement happens, from live video feeds to moving backgrounds to dynamic logos.

The first wave of Gen Xers cut their teeth on video games like Pong, Asteroids, and Pac-Man, but such visual gaming is tame compared to Grand Theft Auto, Call of Duty, and Zelda. The Nintendo Wii revolutionized experiential gaming, while Xbox and Sony PlayStations pushed video games into cyber culture. Virtual reality is now a training tool. In 2013, Google glasses debuted and personalized eyewear that serves as a camera, GPS, clock, and virtual window to the world.

The 2014 Sochi Winter Olympics was a high-definition visual experience. Slow-motion, telephoto, and personal camcorder technology opened a new interface to sports television. Viewers could experience what it was like to luge, speed skate, and ski jump. Up-close camera angles, particularly in slow motion, revealed the reality of every spray of ice, every bead of sweat, and every drop of blood. High definition never looked so good or felt so real. Sochi also decentralized video productions, as fan cams instantly posted winning runs hours before NBC could show the contests in primetime.

The eyes have it. Can you see me now?

Television was the earliest of the postmodern mega-techs, but the innovation of the Internet and cellphone were equally influential in reshaping cultural languages.

On March 12, 2014, the Internet celebrated its silver anniversary. A Pew Research study documented its impact upon culture and the findings are dramatic. Between 1995 and 2014, the use of the Web by the American populace skyrocketed from 14 percent to 81 percent, and more than two-thirds now connect to the Internet with a mobile device.[11]

The Internet first emerged, theoretically, in August 1962 at the Massachusetts Institute of Technology. In 1969, ARPANET was born and enabled primitive networking among four select universities, mostly in California. The first email message was sent in 1972, and a decade later the Internet was clearly established among computer geeks, researchers, developers, and even the military. In 1990, the "www" for World Wide Web was coined, but the most significant Internet date is probably October 13, 1994. That's the day Netscape Navigator was released as a free download. Now anyone could surf the Web.

The Internet revolutionized a Gutenberg culture. Two of the earliest e-retailers were Amazon and eBay (1995), but it's startling to think how quickly life has changed in less than two decades:

- Craigslist, Classmates.com (1995)
- Hotmail (1996)
- Google Search, Yahoo Groups, PayPal (1998)
- Napster (1999)

- Wikipedia (2001)
- LinkedIn, MySpace, Skype, iTunes, WordPress (2003)
- Facebook, Podcast, Flickr (2004)
- YouTube, Reddit, Blogster, Google Earth (2005)
- Twitter (2006)
- Google Street View, Kindle e-reader (2007)
- Amazon Elastic Compute Cloud, DropBox, Spotify (2008)
- Bing, Google Docs, Kickstarter (2009)
- Instagram (2010)
- Google+ social networking, Pinterest (2011)
- Vine (2012)

The technology required to interact with these websites is equally impressive. It's why I've labeled the youngest generation (born since 2005) as the "iTech" generation. They are growing up with smartphones and iPads, streaming video and GPS tracking. They've been cyber-suckled from birth and manipulate touch technology like true digital natives.

The Internet connects all of us, all the time, anywhere there's access. One day the entire globe will be one big WI-FI hotspot.

Of course, the cellphone is a final mega-tech that's equally impressive for the changes it brings. Remember those 1980s "brick" phones? Today's cellphone is truly intelligent and slowly bringing other technologies, including television, music players, GPS, laptops, books, and cameras into one solitary unit. Your phone can show a movie, offer directions, and video a special moment.

According to a Pew Research Center study, 9 in 10 Americans now own a cellphone (compared with 53 percent in 2000), and 58 percent of these phones are "smart" (up 23 percent between 2011 and 2014).[12]

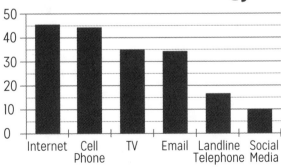

"Must Have" Technology

Chart recreated from Pew Research Center Internet Project Study (2014). Reveals the "percentage of all adults who say these technologies would be very hard or impossible to give up." http://www.pewinternet.org/2014/02/27/summary-of-findings-3

When I moved to Boise in 2007, I did the unthinkable: Our family of four ditched the landline for individual cellphones. Have you noticed the one constant in your life is your cell number? You can move to a different state, even alter your name, but your number never changes. Text messages are socially acceptable forms of communication. In fact, email is going extinct thanks to IM and texting. Micro-messages, popularized by Twitter, are the norm.

The advent of these three mega-techs—television, Internet and cellphones—has created new cultural languages and a postmodern world. Modern culture was grounded to print and clock technology. Postmodern culture sails upon Web, visual, and mobile technology. It's more fluid and fast. It's accessible 24/7/365. It's also temporary and transparent. I wouldn't invest heavily in hard drive technology. The "cloud" is here and, as a metaphor for change, is there anything more temporary and transparent than a cloud?

Modern cultural languages: *Word. Closed. Passive. Mechanical.*

Postmodern cultural languages: *Image. Open. Experiential. Relational.*

In a clock culture, Isaac Newton theorized a closed, objective universe, but in a Web world, Albert Einstein (clearly a man ahead of his time) proposed an open, relative multiverse. In a Gutenberg world, ink on paper reigned, but in a digital economy, all formats are electronic. Even paper cigarettes are now "vapor"-ized. Every year more digital books are published than printed, most by average Joes and Janes who can't score a book deal.

As the iTech generation socially rises and uses exclusively digital media, older formats will naturally disappear. The millennial generation still prefers books, and that gives many old-school Luddites hope, but their generation was still raised on books (whereas the iTech isn't).[15] I foresee books sharing the same fate as the baseball card. Older books will survive in a digital economy like pre-1980 baseball cards thrive. But iTech kids aren't collecting baseball cards. They prefer to play digital video games instead. Newer cards (and books) will be largely worthless in 20 years.

The times have changed. The wineskins no longer hold water with today's postmodern generations. We need to reimagine our communication strategies.

We need a new wineskin to communicate the ever-fresh Wine of Jesus.

Postmodern generations are interactive, experiential, and image-driven.

And they thirst for a wineskin that reflects those characteristics.

Endnotes

1. David Kinnaman and Gabe Lyons, *Unchristian: What A New Generation Really Thinks About Christianity and Why It Matters* (Grand Rapids: Baker Books, 2007), 18, 24-25.

2. President Barack Obama's January 28, 2014 State of the Union Address drew the smallest television ratings in the past 20 years (20.7). His speech of 65 minutes was largely panned on Facebook and Twitter long before the media pundits posted their reviews. Ironically, President Obama is widely known as a skillful orator, but even his speaking ability didn't draw viewers, particularly those under the age of 50 (http://www.nielsen.com/us/en/newswire/2014/33-3-million-tune-in-to-watch-pres-obamas-state-of-the-union-address.html).

3. Robert P. Jones, Daniel Cox, and Thomas Banchoff, *A Generation in Transition: Religion, Values and Politics Among College-Age Millennials* (Public Religion Research Institute: Berkley Center for Religion, Peace & World Affairs, Georgetown University, 2012), 7-8, 31-33.

4. Scott Thumma, "A Health Checkup of U.S. Churches" presentation (Future of The Church Summit, Loveland, CO, October 23-24, 2012). To download a PowerPoint of Dr. Thumma's research, visit: http://hartfordinstitute.org/church_checkup.html.

5. Section 6: Religion and Values (Pew Research Center, June 4 2012), http://www.people-press.org/2012/06/04/section-6-religion-and-social-values/.

6. Jim Henderson, Todd Hunter, and Craig Spinks, *The Outsider Interviews: A New Generation Speaks Out on Christianity* (Grand Rapids: Baker Books, 2010), 19-20.

7. Terry Goodrich, *Evangelicals Have a Higher Divorce Rate, Baylor Report Says*, Baylor University, February 11, 2014, http://www.baptiststandard.com/news/faith-culture/16093-evangelicals-have-higher-divorce-rates-baylor-report-says.

8. "Camelot" is a term from the legends of King Arthur and represents a perfect place. The term was applied to President Kennedy's brief term (1960-1963), reportedly by his wife, Jacqueline, after his assassination.

9. "Color Televisions," http://www.tvhistory.tv/Color_Households_64-78.JPG.

10. Leonard Sweet writes: "In an emerging World Wide Web Society we are seeing a similar massive shift in cultural formation from rational to experiential (E), from representative to participatory (P), from word-based to image-based (I), and from neither individual nor communal to a hybrid of both called connective (C). I call this native consciousness EPIC." *Carpe Manana: Is Your Church Ready To Seize Tomorrow?* (Grand Rapids: Zondervan Publishing, 2001), 33.

11. "The Web at 25 in the U.S." by the Pew Research Center, http://www.pewinternet.org/2014/02/27/summary-of-findings-3/.

12. Ibid.

13. Kevin O'Kelly argued in a Huffington Post blog: "Could those of us who remember the pre-Internet world take a collective breath and calm down? The physical book is alive and well. Book sale statistics show purchasers of e-books buy printed books as well. A recent market survey found readers under 24, the so-called 'digital natives,' actually prefer printed books to e-books," December 26, 2013, http://www.huffingtonpost.com/kevin-okelly/post_6535_b_4504959.html.

THE CALF PATH

One day, through the primeval wood,
A calf walked home, as good calves should;
But made a trail all bent askew,
A crooked trail as all calves do.

Since then two hundred years have fled,
And, I infer, the calf is dead.
But still he left behind his trail,
And thereby hangs my moral tale.

The trail was taken up next day
By a lone dog that passed that way;
And then a wise bell-wether sheep
Pursued the trail o'er vale and steep,
And drew the flock behind him, too,
As good bell-wethers always do.

And from that day, o'er hill and glade,
Through those old woods a path was made;
And many men wound in and out,
And dodged, and turned, and bent about
And uttered words of righteous wrath

Because 'twas such a crooked path.
But still they followed—do not laugh—
The first migrations of that calf,
And through this winding wood-way stalked,
Because he wobbled when he walked.

This forest path became a lane,
That bent, and turned, and turned again;
This crooked lane became a road,
Where many a poor horse with his load
Toiled on beneath the burning sun,
And traveled some three miles in one.
And thus a century and a half
They trod the footsteps of that calf.

The years passed on in swiftness fleet,
The road became a village street,
And this, before men were aware,
A city's crowded thoroughfare;
And soon the central street was this
Of a renowned metropolis;
And men two centuries and a half
Trod in the footsteps of that calf.

Each day a hundred thousand rout
Followed the zigzag calf about;
And o'er his crooked journey went
The traffic of a continent.
A hundred thousand men were led
By one calf near three centuries dead.
They followed still his crooked way,
And lost one hundred years a day;
For thus such reverence is lent
To well-established precedent.

A moral lesson this might teach,
Were I ordained and called to preach;
For men are prone to go it blind
Along the calf-paths of the mind,
And work away from sun to sun
To do what other men have done.
They follow in the beaten track,
And out and in, and forth and back,
And still their devious course pursue,
To keep the path that others do.

But how the wise old wood-gods laugh,
Who saw the first primeval calf!
Ah! many things this tale might teach—
But I am not ordained to preach.

—Sam Walter Foss (1858-1911)

Chapter Three:
THINK DIFFERENT

"When Jesus had finished saying these things, the crowds were amazed at his teaching, because he taught as one who had authority, and not as their teachers of the law."

—Matthew 7:28-29

"A person can have the greatest idea in the world—completely different and novel—but if that person can't convince enough other people, it doesn't matter."

—Gregory Berns[1]

Steve Jobs was a man on a mission to "make a dent in the universe."[2]

Today he is remembered as one of the most influential persons in history.

The Apple story started in the mid-1970s when Jobs hooked up with fellow geek Steve Wozniak. The vision was simple: to create a personal, portable computer. After years of alterations and improvements, the Macintosh computer was revealed to the American public via an infamous 1984 Super Bowl commercial. The age of the desktop computer was underway, and Jobs pioneered a digital revolution.

His charisma was infectious. He even enticed Pepsi CEO John Sculley to leave New York and move cross-country to lead Apple. He did so with a simple almost-messianic pitch: "Do you want to spend the rest of your life selling sugared water, or do you want a chance to change the world?"[3]

Sculley bit the Apple and moved to Palo Alto in 1983.

Ironically, a year later Jobs' own board and the man he hired terminated Steve Jobs. The bitter departure only refocused Jobs. In 1986 he founded a new computer company named NeXt as well as Pixar Animation Studios, the latter of which found tremendous success, including the production of a full-length feature titled *Toy Story*. Meanwhile, without Jobs, Apple computers limped along, watching Microsoft commandeer and control the IBM personal computer market.

Eventually Apple cried uncle, and the Apple board persuaded Steve Jobs to return and lead the company that once kicked him to the curb. When Jobs assumed the helm of the embattled Apple in 1997, it was failing fast and only 90 days from bankruptcy.[4] Steve never lost faith in the Apple product. Despite poor sales in a Windows world, those who purchased Apple computers were rabid fans. By 1998, under Jobs' inspirational leadership, a profit started to show. Nevertheless, Apple computers could muster only 4 percent of the computer market.[5] The late 1990s dot-com bust only worsened matters.

Shortly after returning to Apple, Steve Jobs mustered his tech troops and issued a new edict. It was time to "think different." Basically, Jobs preached it wasn't about building a better computer. Apple already did that (they all believed in their product). He wanted his team to "think different" and beyond boxes. Jobs even narrated a 1997 "Think Different" commercial honoring the "crazy ones" who "see things differently."

In the mid-1990s, MP3 technology was finding traction. Jobs was aware of what digitization had done to photography and so he quietly pursued building a better MP3 player. He wanted something beautiful. Something cool. Something different. Something unrelated to the personal computer and yet desperately synched to it.

1997 "Think Different" Apple Commercial

"Here's to the crazy ones. The misfits. The rebels. The troublemakers. The round pegs in the square holes. The ones who see things differently...They push the human race forward...While some see them as the crazy ones, we see genius. Because the people who are crazy enough to think they can change the world, are the ones who do."[6]

It took a few years, but when the iPod debuted October 23, 2001, it completely changed the MP3 jukebox market. Apple's fortunes rose quickly and overnight became a cultural darling. The reinvigorated computer company didn't rest on its laurels. Rather, under Jobs, Apple used its new cultural moxie to reinvent other technologies like the phone, camera, e-reader, and tablet. Apple also normalized cloud technology.

Today, Apple products remain trendy and the choice for digital entertainment and work. In fact, Apple desktop and laptop sales skyrocketed, and more people now buy an Apple iPad than any other tablet—Apple controls 80 percent of the U.S. market in tablet technology.[7]

Apple beat IBM by thinking different. They built new wineskins that synched better with an Apple computer. Behind every change was the master communicator Steve Jobs.

Carmine Gallo penned, "Steve Jobs is the most captivating communicator on the world stage. No one else comes close. A Jobs presentation unleashes a rush of dopamine into the brains of his audience."[8] His audiences endured long lines and all-night vigils to enjoy prime seating for another Steve talk. Fervent fans even threatened a boycott when they learned Jobs, in failing health from pancreatic cancer, would no longer keynote the 2009 Macworld Expo.

Steve Jobs, who eventually passed away October 5, 2011, clearly made a dent in the universe he sought. To this day, his speaking style is studied, copied, and written about. My YouTube search of "Steve Jobs presentations" yielded 574,000 videos! Only a long view of history will prove Steve Jobs' legacy, but there's little doubt that he reinvented communication.

Two thousand years ago another man was on a mission.

Jesus was a captivating teacher and engaging speaker. Crowds numbering in the thousands followed him and hung on every word—perhaps something not seen before in human history. Jesus used parables, objects, metaphors, and experiences to communicate his message. He spoke on hilltops, inside synagogues, around tables, and along shorelines—completely outside the box. His hearers were a motley mix of spiritual seekers, zealots, misfits, and socially unacceptable outsiders. Nevertheless, Jesus equally and easily connected with the religious elite Nicodemus and the street-wise Mary Magdalene; the affluent young leader and the Roman centurion; the tax collector and the fisherman.

Jobs made a dent in the universe, but Jesus changed the world. And they both accomplished their missions through creative communication contextualized to their culture. Jobs preached, "Think different." Jesus preached, "Be different." To critics they were crazy, but to their disciples they were captivating. The difference? I doubt we'll quote Jobs in a thousand years, nor define history around his life (BJ/AJ). Jobs was a visionary, but he was no messiah. Even still, we can learn from his style.

Both Jesus and Steve Jobs recognized that communication boils down to three essential elements: the messenger, the message, and the method. The beauty emerges within their triune nature. Each part flows and interacts with the others. They are fluid. The who, what, and how are connected and communal. Whether it's a 30-second elevator speech or 60-minute keynote presentation or a 25-minute Sunday sermon, communication demands all three to dance in unison.

WATERING DOWN THE MESSAGE

Our world is mostly fluid.

Seventy percent of the globe is covered in H_2O, and 97 percent of all the water on earth is oceanic salt water. Water is essential to life. A man can live three weeks without food, but it only takes three to five days for dehydration to kill. Up to two-thirds of the human body is water.

We are water people living in a wet world.

The fluidity of postmodern culture only magnifies the incapability of modern communication containers. The famous preacher Dwight L. Moody was known for continually asking God to "fill him up." When asked why, he simply answered, "Because I leak."[9] In a fluid culture, we need methods that hold water with emerging generations. The messenger will leak (because he or she is fissured with imperfections). The message will leak (because it's born out of bias and subjectivity). And the method will leak (because no communication strategy is sacred).

For centuries the modern world was grounded in objectivity, propositions, reason, and one-way communication. The homily or sermon was a perfect strong box to hold the message. In a culture captivated by rationalism, the lecture was a perfect wineskin. The modern mind, grooved by Gutenberg and clock technology, processed information best within boxes. It made sense. I think, therefore I am.

But a fluid postmodern culture sails upon the waters of interactivity, experience, and image. Communication now leaks 24/7/365. Truth is confirmed by personal experience. And if a single image preaches a thousand words (perhaps ten thousand words), then why do preachers keep saying a thousand words when one image will do? The postmodern mind, wired by Web and visual technology, processes information through conversation, environment, and picture. If you feel it, it's true. I experience, therefore I am.

Does that mean the 45-minute Sunday message is history?

Not necessarily.

But the human mind has a short attention span and master communicators have learned not to exhaust their audiences. Thom Schultz penned an insightful blog post about what communicators can discover from children's ministry and offered five practices: keep it simple, make it visual, welcome questions, make it brief, and praise God.[10] I would only add a sixth suggestion: get a laugh.

What we need to do is think differently about "message" time or the fluid 30 to 40 minutes we use to "give a talk." Instead of pouring God's Word into a leaky lecture box and exhausting the time in one-way communication, what if we created a "message experience"? Let's apply Schultz's five strategies straight out of the children's ministry culture to the Sunday sermon and soak it for a postmodern audience.

KEEP IT SIMPLE!

The average sermon is mostly a content dump of information or application, depending on the preacher. Some will wax eloquent on unique words, historical contexts, and right interpretations of the passage. Others will explore only what it means and how it applies. The former impresses the intellect, while the latter inspires the heart. The former reveals insights, while the latter explores ideas. And yet, after a while, both avenues exhaust the hearer and bore the mind. Why? Because the mind wants to do both! It needs to think deeply and find useful purpose for the material.

Bruce Wilkinson argues that we need to "master the minimum." So let's think differently. Instead of an oral content dump for 40 minutes, what if we reinvented our messages into short 10-minute nuggets of insight (like a YouTube teaching video)? It's very important to communicate truth and information, but it can be easily limited. During these teaching segments, you concentrate on the most important facts or insights. Choose one and explore it. We'll talk more about how this is done in Chapter 8.

> Christy wrote: "I know, I know. I KNOW! And yet. When I was eleven, my parents changed churches because of the great preaching. The preacher delivered a deeply researched, finely honed sermon lasting at least a half-hour, and my parents hung on every word—my father usually jotting notes and both parents discussing the message on the way home. It's hard for me to get out of my head that this is what it looks like to teach, lead and motivate the people of God. Of course, that was another day and a different generation."
>
> (A comment on Thom Schultz's blog, *Holy Soup*.)

MAKE IT VISUAL!

The postmodern mind processes in images.

So if you want to speak into the postmodern context you must reinvent your messages as visual metaphors. Following Jesus is like riding in a motorcycle gang. Forgiveness is like a hard rain. Joy is like a Yellowstone geyser. Jesus was a master of visual communication. The Kingdom is like a net (Matthew 13:47). God's Word is like a seed (Matthew 13:1-9). Heaven is like a priceless pearl (Matthew 13:44-46). Hell is like a garbage dump outside of Jerusalem—aka Gehenna (Matthew 5:29).[11] James would liken the tongue to fire or a rudder (James 3:4-6). Even intellectual Paul taught deep theology through metaphor. The law was like being married to a perfectionist (Romans 7:1-6) or under guardianship (Galatians 3:23-28). The church is like a field or building (1 Corinthians 3:5-15) or marriage (Ephesians 5:25-33). The spiritual life is like fruit (Galatians 5:22-23).

We do have one tool, though, that Jesus and Paul did not.

We have the power of video. We can invite our audiences into a living story.

If a picture holds a thousand words, a video clip contains ten thousand words. I always laugh when a preacher illustrates his point with a reference to a film but exhausts more time explaining it to his audience than if he simply showed the clip! We also can use presentation technology (PowerPoint, Keynote, Prezi) to enhance visual potency. We can create visual themed environments and use object lessons.

Recently I listened to a preacher speak on the difference between a full and empty life when one faces trial. To illustrate his point, he held up two soda cans that looked in every way similar. He then pressed hard on both cans. One kept its form and the other crumbled (for it had been drained by a small hole in the bottom). This object lesson was the only thing I remember from his talk!

WELCOME QUESTIONS!

Postmodern culture is constantly talking. Every day more text messages are sent than people living on the planet (a good chunk, no doubt, by my son!). Social media communicates, whether you tweet, post, or upload.

Consequently, a major reinvention will be who's in control of the Sunday message. For the first time in history, the control has shifted from the center to the edges, from the preacher to the people, from the professor to the pupils. In nearly every congregation there are individuals who boast more education, wider experiences, deeper insight, greater ideas, and smoother ability to communicate than you. They are bursting with questions and brimming with comments!

If you've studied your passage, your expertise will gain their respect, but that doesn't mean they have nothing to say. In fact, if they're tech savvy they already posting their thoughts online while you speak. I once watched a 20-something draw while he listened to a lecture. His approach inspired me for the next several weeks to use an iPad app to paint the pastor's sermon then post to Facebook as an act of worship art.

So what if you stopped being the sage from the stage and became the guide from the side? What if every message time contained several opportunities for interactivity? What if you asked more questions and gave fewer answers? What if teaching time looked more like Google Search than Encyclopedia Britannica? What if you operated more like a tour guide?

MAKE IT BRIEF!

The mind can only absorb what the seat can endure.

One of my favorite stories in Acts is when Paul gets a bit windy and causes a man to snooze to his death. In Acts 20:7-12, Paul is reported to have "talked on and on" and dulled a man into a "deep sleep." His slumber got the best of him around midnight, and he fell from the third story window, dying upon impact! Paul, without missing a beat, resurrected the fellow and still "talked until daylight."

I've heard many a preacher use this story to defend *their* long sermons, but I fear they miss the point. First, while Paul did "talk on and on," we don't know if it was continuous. Ancient gatherings often had multiple meals, conversations, and teaching time that lasted many hours, even all day and all night. Even in the text, after the man's resurrection, they have dinner before Paul revs back up again.

Second, it's probable this is an exceptional incident. Paul is leaving the area and hosts an all-night discipleship cram. It's doubtful he preached (or operated) like this all the time. In fact, his only recorded sermons (Acts 13:16-41; 17:22-31; 28:17-20) and speeches (Acts 14:15-17; 20:18-35; 22:1-21; 24:10-21; 26:2-23) are brief.

Paul also argued he'd do anything to anyone using any means available to proclaim God's Word (1 Corinthians 9:21-23). In today's shrinking attention span culture, it's safe to assume Paul would abbreviate his talks.

Enough said.

PRAISE GOD!

The reason we gather as the church is to celebrate and experience God.

We don't gather for a concert. We don't gather for announcements. We don't gather even to give offerings. Nor do we gather for a spiritual lecture.

Now none of these things are necessarily *wrong*, but they're not the reason we connect and commune as the body of Christ. A few years ago, my son and I went to church in Salt Lake City. We arrived early and waited in a line for hours to enter.

Even when the doors opened, we waited several more hours. As we waited, we soaked in the experience with anticipation. We reminisced. We interacted with others. We enjoyed a meal. That night we attended the Church of U2 with tens of thousands of other fans to celebrate and experience music with a message. We sang until hoarse but with a smile and gratitude to finally enjoy the band personally. U2 engineered a truly spiritual, communal experience, and I found myself in worship. However, I wasn't worshipping Bono or the Edge. Rather, I was letting their music and the visuals move me into a Divine Space. I was singing to God. I was feeling God. I was enjoying God.

But isn't that what church should be?

Isn't that the reason we listen? Or sing? Or give?

Bono and Steve Jobs are men on a mission. But their messages pale in comparison to the words of Paul and Jesus, or yours and mine.

Bono and Steve Jobs simply help us understand how we need to think differently and craft spiritual, communal experiences so our message is understood, embraced, and inculcated into life. The message, messenger, and method interact to create Divine Space. The reason Christians gather is to connect and commune with God through Jesus Christ, to rediscover and recommit to Messiah and Mission.

The cattle call Sunday experience at many American churches was never what God intended. The original DNA of the church, as revealed in the book of Acts, was communal, conversational, and catechumenal. The purpose of their gatherings is found in a single verse: "They devoted themselves to the apostles' teaching and to fellowship, to the breaking of bread and to prayer" (Acts 2:42).

Early Christians met to learn, to connect, to commune ("breaking of bread" refers to the Eucharist, or Lord's Supper), and to pray. Did you notice what's missing? No singing, no offerings, and no sermon. Now it doesn't mean they didn't sing or give or listen to preaching, but if these activities did not cause growth in faith, interaction with other Christians, an experiential communion (in body and blood of Christ), or prayer, then it didn't necessarily *have* to happen. The purpose was clear. The strategies were fluid.

Here's the taste test for the Sunday sermon:
- Does it teach truth and inspire life change?
- Does it create interaction and community?
- Does it invite the participant into the Communion experience?
- Does it produce a prayerful response?

- Does it focus upon a simple, single point?
- Is it wrapped within a visual metaphor?
- Is it brief and friendly to short attention spans?
- Is it enjoyable?

In 1997, the Apple computer company was nearly bankrupt. In 2014, the American church is struggling to remain relevant in an increasingly carnal, secular, postmodern culture. The Sunday sermon is out of sync with how we socially communicate. We talk long, but they listen short. We speak words, but they hear images. We communicate one way, but they interact all ways. We demand full attention, but they crave shared conversation.

Unless obsolescence is preferred, we have no choice but to reinvent.

The rest of this book is about how we need to *think different*. After all, we're not selling sugar water either. We're inviting people to immerse themselves in Living Water.

Fluid. Fast. Friendly.

And radically beyond the box.

Endnotes

1. Kathi Baker, "Neuroscientist Reveals How Nonconformists Achieve Success," (Woodruff Health Sciences Center, Emory University, 25 September 2008), http://whsc.emory.edu/press_releases2.cfm?announcement_id_seq=15766.

2. "Quotes on Initiative," *Leadership Now,* http://www.leadershipnow.com/initiativequotes.html.

3. Walter Isaacson, *Steve Jobs* (New York: Simon and Schuster, 2011), 154.

4. Steven Levy, *The Perfect Thing: How the iPod Shuffles Commerce, Culture, and Coolness* (New York: Simon and Schuster, 2006), 87.

5. Ibid, 92.

6. "1984 Apple's Macintosh Commercial," Mac History, https://www.youtube.com/watch?v=VtvjbmoDx-I.

7. "Apple iPad Alternatives: The Competition Finally Heats Up," October 31, 2013, http://www.pcmag.com/slideshow/story/264947/apple-ipad-alternatives-the-competition-finally-heats-up.

8. Carmine Gallo, *The Presentation Secrets of Steve Jobs: How To Be Insanely Great in Front of Any Audience* (New York, NY: McGraw-Hill, 2010), ix.

9. Owen Bourgaize, "DL Moody Was Once Asked Why He Urged Christians..." June, 2001, http://www.sermoncentral.com/illustrations/sermon-illustration-owen-bourgaize-quotes-holyspiritbaptism-loveofthedisciples-2970.asp.

10. Read Thom's blog on children's ministry and communication, "What Children's Ministry Can Teach Grown-Up Church," http://holysoup.com/2014/02/18/what-childrens-ministry-can-teach-grown-up-church/.

11. Most translations use "hell" instead of "Gehenna." Historically, Gehenna was a garbage dump outside of Jerusalem that burned continuously. So when Jesus referred to spiritual punishment as similar to Gehenna, it evoked repugnant smells and feelings.

Chapter Four:
CAN YOU HEAR ME NOW?

"How, then, can they call on the one they have not believed in? And how can they believe in the one of whom they have not heard? And how can they hear without someone preaching to them? And how can anyone preach unless they are sent? As it is written: 'How beautiful are the feet of those who bring good news!'"

—Romans 10:14-15

Can you hear me now?

For years this catchy pitch phrase branded Verizon wireless phone service. After all, one of the major disruptions in early cellphone use was the dropped call or "missing bars." Actually, it still is. On a recent road trip to eastern Oregon I had to cut short an engaging conversation due to "skip" (a frustrating cellular condition that results in hearing every third word). Despite a temptation to curse my cellphone to wireless Hades, I knew it wasn't the phone's fault. The problem was my provider. I was out of touch, off the grid, and in the skip.

Can you (silence) me now?

Sometimes I wonder if God doesn't feel the same about the Sunday sermon.

God desperately hungers to communicate and commune with his people, but his cell service (you and me) is spotty, weak, or nonexistent. We aren't connected to culture, so our illustrations ring hollow and irrelevant. Our research of the Scriptures is weak, so our insights are few and superficial. Our applications are spotty, so people walk away without life-changing direction. Our communication strategies are old school, so younger audiences quickly bore.

The problem with our call is our connection.

THE CALL IS FOR YOU

The first step in communicating God's Word is to be anointed for the task. Originally, this was the meaning of ordination. In the early church, leaders and missionaries were set apart for ministry (Acts 6:1-6; 13:1-3). You couldn't buy an ordination paper. You couldn't earn it. It wasn't even up for vote. You were appointed and anointed by your immediate faith community.

God validated Jesus at his baptism with the actual words every student heard from his rabbi mentor in his graduation blessing: "This is my Son, whom I love; with him I am well pleased" (Matthew 3:17). Later God repeated his blessing and added three crucial words: "Listen to him!" (Matthew 17:5). Essentially, Jesus was called and recalled.

> "While he was still speaking, a bright cloud covered them, and a voice from the cloud said, "This is my Son, whom I love; with him I am well pleased. Listen to him!'"
>
> —Matthew 17:5

That's why we can't talk preaching strategy until we've talked about your heart. *Why are you doing this? What's your motivation to communicate God's Word? Do you sense a calling to preach?* Those may be pointed questions, but that's the point. Ultimately, preaching is a spiritual enterprise. Any warm body can talk, and most communicators can master strategies to inspire and inform, but preaching isn't about us, it's really about God. We're simply vessels. We're the cellphone. If our calling (provider) is spotty and there are large gaps in our spiritual motivation, then people won't hear the message. We'll drop a lot of calls (not to mention credibility). Our words will be like dust in the wind. Our strategies, no matter how creative, will fail.

The call to preach is different for every person.

But perhaps it looks a lot like Samuel. In 1 Samuel 3, a young man heard God utter his name in the dead of night. According to the passage, "The word of the Lord was rare in those days" (3:1). Translation: The calls were few and far between. But God found a boy with his heart asleep in the "house of the Lord" (3:3). Samuel wasn't highly educated or experienced (yet). He didn't have pedigree, popularity, or power. But he knew where God dwelt, and that's where he laid his head. Smart kid.

Can you hear me now?

Good.

Samuel's calling didn't just happen by accident. Samuel's heart was right. His motivations were pure. His desires were holy. When God talked, Samuel listened. In fact, his calling (and ours) follows a very predictable path: Can. You. Hear. Me. Now.

CAN = THE WILL

Every calling begins as a moment of divine stickiness. It's wired by a passionate pursuit to remain in the presence of Christ in order to be glued to God's purpose and power. Too often, we don't experience Christ or hear God because we are nowhere near him. We prefer to be part-time prophets. Or we permeate our lives with the noise of busyness. Or we don't feel worthy or wanted. Or, worse, we don't even think God cares. Most of these thoughts are rooted to the will. We lack motivation, willpower, or positive God-esteem.

Rich Mullins once penned, "Christ does not promise His filling to those who have an appetite for righteousness or even for those who have a craving for it. He promises filling to those whose

> "I am the vine; you are the branches. If you remain in me and I in you, you will bear much fruit; **apart from me you can do nothing**."
>
> —John 15:5

survival is dependent on it. For these people—for such a person—'to do the will of their Father is their bread and water.' They know that to live they must do."[1]

The central question is "can?" Can you draw closer to God? Can you eliminate the commotion of culture? Can you release your fear and regret? Can you passionately pursue holiness? Can you purposely seek the heart of God? Can you confess that God is truly crazy about you?

Can you? Absolutely you can. It's a matter of the will.

Samuel didn't have to park his bed near the Ark of the Covenant or sleep close to God. He could have slept near his mentor Eli. Perhaps it was his youthful idealism that inspired him to plant his sleeping bag where he did. After all, Samuel was young and optimistic. It's an important insight, because some of the most jaded preachers I know are older. When you're young you don't know what you don't know. The older you get, the more reality sours optimism. You preach up a storm and only make waves. You burn with passion and leave only smelling of smoke. You speak with power and purpose and hear only groans, grumbles, and gripes.

I know, because I've been there.

But I didn't stay there.

And whenever I start feeling jilted or jaded, I remember Ezekiel and the valley of dry bones (Ezekiel 37:1-14). Now that was a dead audience. Nevertheless, God called Ezekiel to prophesy to them, and shortly the bones rattled and connected, then tendons and flesh emerged, and finally skin appeared. Miraculously, a whole army stood on its feet after God breathed into them *life*. The fact that Ezekiel spoke to the bones at all is what's amazing to me. I would've been tempted to turn around and go home. Preach to a bone yard? Seriously God? I wonder if I could prophesy with much passion or power in a cemetery. Why waste my time and talent talking to the dead? Mediocrity has muffled—even muzzled—many a called prophet.

We see dry bones.

> *God sees a living army.*

We see the end.

> *God sees a beginning.*

We see failure.

> *God sees success.*

We see death.

> *God sees resurrection.*

And every opportunity invites a single word wired to your will: *can.*

YOU = INVITATION

The second part of calling is accepting a divine invitation into what God is actually doing. God summons, but we must answer. We may have the want to follow but not the commitment. We may desire to go where God is leading but remain riddled with excuses. We may wish to preach but question our ability.

Jeremiah was like that.

God beckoned this young prophet with these tender, maternal words: "Before I formed you in the womb, I knew you, before you were born I set you apart; I appointed you as a prophet to the nations" (Jeremiah 1:5). The invitation wasn't debatable, but the acceptance was. Jeremiah played the "age card" and pointed out he's too young for the job. *Maybe I'll go later but not now.* He argued his inexperience. He hadn't passed a public speaking course. He's too young to join Toastmasters. God must have targeted the wrong kid. *Maybe I'll prophesy later but not now.* God wasn't shaken by Jeremiah's protest.

But that's what makes God...well...*God!*

Isn't it odd how God loves to validate the invalid, anoint the average, and ordain those whom society deems inoperative, insignificant, or ignorant? Jeremiah was just a kid, while Moses had one foot in the geriatric ward. Face it, you're never too young, too old, or too *anything* for God. To paraphrase Yoda: *Do or do not, there is no try.* Before you can preach the supernatural Word of God, you must be wholly persuaded by God's invitation that you, and you alone, are the mouthpiece for his message. "Can *YOU?*" Can you speak what I need spoken? Can you live what you will preach? Can you handle the critic? Preaching is more than giving a speech. It's an invitation to partner with God without question or reservation.

Yes, God will invite others. But he has especially selected *you.*

HEAR = SKILL AND ABILITY

The third part of calling involves skill and ability.

Can you *hear?*

Sometimes God does prefer innocence and ignorance, so he calls a Samuel or Jeremiah. But more often than not, he needs an experienced, educated individual for the job. The Apostle Paul was a "chosen instrument" (Acts 9:15). In order to interact with a pagan Greco-Roman culture, God needed an educated and experienced religious fanatic. Someone who'd kill to get the job done or be killed doing it. Peter, John, and the other apostles were good guys, but they lacked both education and experience. They enjoyed hanging at home. God needed a guy with a passport.

> "But the Lord said to Ananias, 'Go! **This man is my chosen instrument** to proclaim my name to the Gentiles and their kings and to the people of Israel.'"
>
> —Acts 9:15

Moses was another highly educated leader. According to Acts 7:22, he was schooled in "all the wisdom of the Egyptians." When God called Moses through ancient burning bush technology (Exodus 3), he was far more cynical than Samuel. He was on the lam working with lambs. One day he witnessed a flaming shrub in the distance. This wasn't unusual. Bushes burn all the time in the Sinai desert. This one, however, wasn't burning up nor was the fire spreading. Moses was naturally captivated (perhaps he studied Egyptian stuff like pyrotechnics and pyramids). God used a natural event to issue a supernatural calling.

For most of us, this is how God speaks into our lives. A natural event is soaked with divine opportunity. We simply live life. We get an education. We go to work. We get married and raise a family. And then something happens. God puts a fiery shrub within eyeshot. It captivates. It calls. It even commands.

Erwin McManus calls these "divine moments" and contends: "The most spiritual activity you will engage in today is making choices. All the other activities that we describe as spiritual—worship, prayer, meditation—are there to connect us to God and prepare us to live. While moments are the context within which we live, choices chart the course and determine the destination."[2]

Moses had a choice. He could've ignored the flame but, like Paul, he was a chosen instrument. Moses was uniquely qualified to lead the Israelites out of Egypt. He spent his first four decades walking like an Egyptian and the next forty years herding his father-in-law's flocks in the desert. God needed someone who smelled like sheep but could stand up to a pharaoh, someone who had a wilderness survival merit badge but also Egyptian schooling.

> "In times of change, learners inherit the earth, while the learned find themselves beautifully equipped to deal with a world that no longer exists."[3]
>
> —Eric Hoffer

Can you *hear?*

God desperately needs skilled communicators. He values education and experience. The good news in a 21st century digital Web world is you don't need an academic degree to make the grade. But you must be an insatiable learner. Leaders are readers, and communicators are consumers. They boast a voracious appetite and satiate themselves with stories, anecdotes, quotes, factoids, and insights. You can't lead where you haven't been nor speak about what you don't know. When you listen and learn about theology, history, psychology, philosophy, science, sociology, languages, and culture, you grow deep and wide with insight and ideas.

If communicators aren't careful, they can deafen to the world outside.

First they ignore opportunities to learn. Then they muffle influences that invoke new material. Then they silence everything but their own imagination. I once asked a preacher (known for his boring messages) how he prepared to preach. He told me on Saturday night he opened up his Bible to the selected text (picked on Friday in order to get the bulletin to print!) and read the passage three times, then he prayed and asked the Holy Spirit to speak through him.

His messages were dry, void of imagination and illustration, and largely ineffective. He missed the stories in his faith community. He was deaf to cultural events and people to build relevant bridges. He was even woefully ignorant of theology, relying on what he knew (which wasn't much).

It's not really *can you hear* but *do you hear?*

And there are only two keys to unlock crystal clear hearing (both work best in tandem): education and experience. Education without experience breeds intellectualism. Experience without education spawns superficiality. Master communicators learn and love both.

ME = DIVINE COMMISSION

The fourth facet of calling is the commission. It's "where" God is sending the called. But buckle in (tight), because it's highly doubtful you'll like the destination. Peter was told he would die someplace he'd never imagine. Maybe that's why I always chuckle when people say God told them to do this or do that. Not because God talked to them, but because they seem rather giddy about the assignment. Now, obviously, God works within our desires and sometimes his calling matches our wishes.

> "Very truly I tell you, when you were younger you dressed yourself and went where you wanted; but when you are old you will stretch out your hands, and someone else will dress you and lead you **where you do not want to go**.' Jesus said this to indicate the kind of death by which Peter would glorify God. Then he said to him, **'Follow me!'"**
>
> —John 21:18-19

But if you're going to preach God's Word and you are open to God's commission, then resign yourself to a life of doubt and difficulty. God once told me to give away my car to a needy family. I know it was God because there's no way I would've thought that thought! Thankfully, I obeyed. God was already working, and before nightfall I had another vehicle (completely paid for within a month!). That's the way God works. When he talks, your first response is "no!"

Just ask Jonah.

He was commissioned to go to Ninevah. He had the tools and the openness to serve God. He just didn't want to go *there*. He was a small town prophet. So he did what a lot of pastors do when push comes to shove: Jonah jumped ship. He ran from the clear call of God. His "no" produced one whale of a journey, first as shark bait, and then as indigestion, and finally a rather rude dumping on a beach outside Ninevah. Can you imagine the sight? After three days soaking in stomach acid, Jonah's skin would've been bleached white and puckered, his hair gone, and dressed in little more than threadbare attire and seaweed. It's no wonder the Ninevites repented!

Moses didn't appreciate his commission either.

And God was not impressed. Moses stuttered an excuse that he flunked speech and had stage fright. He pouted, *Who am I to do the job?*, and sulked about nobody listening.

> "This truth is consistent to life itself: the greatest opportunities require the highest risk. If we want to live life to the fullest, we must be willing to trust God and risk everything."[4]
>
> —Erwin McManus, *Seizing Your Divine Moment*

Finally, he cut to the chase: *God, send someone else! I think you fingered the wrong shepherd. Besides, I'm too old for mission impossible.* Moses had every right to question God. He was old. He did stutter. He was just a Sinai shepherd. And let's not forget the reason he's camped in the desert for four decades: He's an Egyptian felon on the run. He's on wanted posters in every post office from Cairo to Alexandria.

You see, when God calls your first response is no. And you'll probably have plenty of excuses too. Some of you reading this book simply can't see yourself preaching. You're introverted. You don't like public speaking. You're scared you'll say something stupid. But deep down you said "yes!" to God's commission.

And here you are.

The good news is God works far better with fear than pride. If you trust the process, God will strengthen your confidence. He has a much harder time with the arrogant who feel they've already arrived. I was that type of guy. My homiletics professor struggled to teach this former high school speech champion. I was pretty cocky. I was like another homiletics student who was informed by his teacher that he was a "model" preacher. The compliment fueled his pride until he looked up the word "model" in the dictionary and learned it was a "cheaper imitation of the real thing."

Can you hear *Me?*

God both calls and commissions his servants. You're not just preaching words. You're preaching His Words. You're not simply addressing people. You are speaking to His People. Every time you preach, you are God's voice. It doesn't matter if there are five or fifty or five thousand people. You're God's man or woman.

And with God, everything is possible.

NOW = SETTING

The final portion of a calling is the context.

It's Jonah in Ninevah. It's Moses in Pharaoh's courts. It's Jeremiah, Ezekiel, and Isaiah boldly prophesying to a hard-hearted, dull, and deaf crowd. It's Timothy busting his pastoral butt in Ephesus and getting no respect. This may be the most difficult part of a calling. It's one thing to be open to God's will or get educated for the work or even go where he's commanded.

It's another matter to stay put.

It's tough to preach every week. It's challenging to craft a message that communicates every Sunday. It's a pain to research a passage, study strategies, and invest hours into a sermon that'll be over in half an hour. Most (popular) professional speakers have only a few "canned" messages. It's an industry trade secret: three and out. Create three fantastic speeches and rent a fast car. Get in. Get out.

> "Watch your life and doctrine closely. **Persevere** in them, because if you do, you will save both yourself and your hearers."
> —1 Timothy 4:16

That's why I admire anyone who accepts the call to preach. And then lets people record it, even broadcast it in Web-land.

Can you hear me *now?*

Good.

We all preach in a unique context. Those who congregate on Sunday bring to the auditorium their own stories, troubles, baggage, and experiences. Nowhere else on earth will that same group exist in that space and time. It's why I hesitate to be overly prescriptive. What succeeds in Sarasota won't necessarily sell in Seattle. And what fails in Minneapolis might be a hit in Memphis. But it's deeper than that. Your context is unique in your own city. Your people are distinct from all other churches in your community.

Can you hear me *now?*

One size no longer fits all. The preaching strategies to come are fluid. That means they are adaptable, flexible, and moldable. Some might work without any change. Others might need tweaking. Still some might require wholesale change. A few might not be for you at all.

Can you hear me now?

Good.

I hate dropped calls. And God isn't much for them either.

STAYING THE COURSE

Perhaps you wonder why a divine calling is so essential to preaching.

It's because when we soak our souls in our calling, we unleash power, persistence, and potential. I've been a ministry professor for more than two decades and taught thousands of students the finer points of pastoral ministry. Some of my best students in academic performance, particularly those skilled in communication, were the first to forsake their calling. In contrast, I taught far more average students who proved and improved their devotion to pastoral leadership because they couldn't run from their call.

Can. You. Hear. Me. Now?

You might as well stop reading at this point if you don't sense some fire in your bones to speak the Living Words of a Holy God. If your soul isn't heated white hot to devour and deliver Scripture with fresh insight and bold ideas, then you probably won't last. If you won't be radically transparent in your own spiritual journey—both the success and the failure—then your preaching will fall upon deaf ears, especially the postmodern generations.

That's why we need to reimagine the sermon.

People don't want another spiritual lecture. They desire to experience God. If you can't lose your own mask and get real with people, who will? If you can't go deep into God's Word in your own study, then why would you expect people want to pursue biblical maturity? If you can't be culturally in tune, then what are you saying about living life Monday through Saturday?

> "But if I say, 'I will not mention his word or speak anymore in his name,' his word is in my heart like a fire, a fire shut up in my bones. I am weary of holding it in; indeed, I cannot."
>
> —Jeremiah 20:9

Maybe your heart to preach burns like Jeremiah. He passionately proclaimed that God's Word was raging fire within his heart. It's an inspirational quip for a poster, but have you ever read Jeremiah 20? The prophet is in pain. Jeremiah starts by calling God out as a deceiver (verse 7). He complains everyone mocks and insults him (verse 8). That's when he taps that inner passion to speak God's Word. Unfortunately, it doesn't last. His critics are getting louder and even his friends wait for him to mess up (verse 10). In verses 11-13, Jeremiah briefly sings praise before falling back into depression to curse the day he was born (verses 14-18).

But Jeremiah was the real deal. And people listen to a prophet who's an open book. They follow a preacher who has an open heart. They model a person who's an open life.

The number one human quality people hunger for today is *authenticity*. They want you to be real. Real with yourself. Real with God. Real with them. And the only way to authenticate a life and stay real is with an undeniable, insatiable, outrageous embrace of your calling, even if it hurts like heck.

There's no one else like you. You're one of a kind. You're one of a call.

PREACHING WITH POWER!

You want to preach like Jeremiah?

Then learn, love, and live this simple outline once uttered by an old yet wise preacher when asked his secret to preaching:

First, I reads myself full,

then I thinks myself clear,

then I prays myself hot,

then I lets myself go!

To this day, I believe this statement possesses the four essential ingredients to power preaching.

PREPARATION *("FIRST, I READS MYSELF FULL...")*

If you don't prepare, you will repair.

Simply, the more ready you are to speak, the less likely you will experience problems. Preparation involves study of the passage (historical, linguistic, theological, cultural contexts). It means you develop a strategy to remember the message. How will you preach so the people won't forget it? It's an important question.

Preparation involves knowing your audience. Even if you've been preaching to the same crowd for years, how well do you know what's happening in their lives? Every individual and every family has emotional baggage, good and bad. You also need to know your community and culture. When a major news story impacts your congregation (local, national, or international), how can you use it to build a bridge?

Finally, preparation means resolving presentation issues. Think through every scenario. If something could go wrong, how could you prevent it? How many messages have been soured by poor preparation? A video clip that won't play right. A misspelled word on the PowerPoint. A dry mouth and throat that erupts into a coughing fit. An illustration poorly communicated. Stuff happens when you speak. And one of the reasons I know there's a spiritual enemy is because things especially happen to God's spokespersons. Anyone called to preach the Word has a target on his or her back.

PURPOSE *("THEN I THINKS MYSELF CLEAR...")*

The second secret to power preaching is one-point communication. Master communicators and professional speakers have learned this strategy well. What's the golden nugget in your message? Boil content to the irreducible minimum. Sift your sermon until there's a single point.

And then repeat it over and over again.

Some schools of preaching call this the dominant thought, while others refer to it as the big idea. Regardless of term, every message needs a centralizing statement to supply traction of insight and movement in application.

We'll talk more about how you do this with postmodern generations in future chapters.

PRAYER *("THEN I PRAYS MYSELF HOT...")*

A third component is the one most tragically overlooked. I know, because I'm often guilty of a lack of prayer. Once your message is finished, you need to bathe it in prayer. Ask God to bless, protect, and inspire. Invite the Holy Spirit to speak where you can't or fail. Pray over your people and, specifically, for open hearts, minds, and lives. Petition God to protect your technology (visual, audio) and your voice (physical). Finally, seek God's favor by pursuing what's right, just, and honorable. God needs a clear and clean connection.

PASSION *("THEN I LETS MYSELF GO...")*

If you've properly prepared, if your message travels upon a single dominant thought, and if you've thoroughly soaked everything in prayer, don't be surprised if God shows up. It's a bit like Shadrach, Meshach, and Abednego in the fiery furnace. They held true to their faith, and God showed up. You've heard of the sixth man in basketball and the twelfth man in football? These three Jewish guys experienced the Fourth Man.

A few insights on letting yourself go.

First, be yourself. Remember, God has called you uniquely to this task. You may not feel capable, but if you've prepared properly, God will use your words. Stop the comparison game. Are there better speakers? Yes. You may be the best, award-winning speaker in the world, but you'll eventually discover there's still someone better. Just be *you*.

Second, preach from your heart. Effective communication isn't a head trip. It's a heart thing. People remember how you made them feel. Trust me, they'll forget your insights. Even if they take notes, they'll lose them in time or tragedy. Nothing lasts forever except the Word of God. So speak it, heart to heart.

Finally, be enthusiastic. The word *enthusiasm* is rooted in two Greek words: *en* (translation: in) and *theos* (translation: God). Literally, to be enthusiastic is to be in God! Enthusiasm reveals itself in a smile or a gesture or a movement. Enthusiasm emerges in your voice. God's Word has you, and you have no other choice but to speak God's Word! You can't wait to preach. You must preach. Now *that's* passion.

You will never preach with power unless you're called. God doesn't use vessels he hasn't tested, taught, and transformed.

Can you hear me now?

Good.

Endnotes

1. James Bryan Smith, *Rich Mullins: A Devotional Biography: An Arrow Point To Heaven* (Nashville, TN: Broadman & Holman, 2000), 251.

2. Erwin McManus, *Seizing Your Divine Moment* (Nashville, TN: Thomas Nelson, 2002), 19.

3. Eric Hoffer, as quoted by Leonard Sweet, *AquaChurch 2.0* (Colorado Springs, CO: David C. Cook, 2008), 302.

4. Erwin McManus, *Seizing Your Divine Moment* (Nashville, TN: Thomas Nelson, 2002), 134.

Chapter Five:
STARFISH

"In the last days, God says, I will pour out my Spirit on all people. Your sons and daughters will prophesy, your young men will see visions, your old men will dream dreams. Even on my servants, both men and women, I will pour out my Spirit in those days, and they will prophesy."

—Acts 2:17-18

Happy Days was one of my favorite childhood shows.

This mid-70s retro-comedy launched one of television's most iconic figures: Arthur Fonzarelli, or the Fonz. Fonzie was a leather-clad, motorcycle-bound hooligan who got all the girls, terrified all the guys, and radiated coolness by the gallon. His broad toothy smile, slicked back shock, and trademark "aaaaaaay" were mimicked by wannabe mini-Fonzies everywhere. The Fonz could do no wrong.

Except for one thing.

He couldn't actually say the word "wrong."

Even when caught in a moment of mistake, the Fonz would struggle to say the word. His heart and mind knew the truth, but his tongue wouldn't cooperate. He'd mumble out something unintelligible instead. It was simply wrong for the Fonz to be *wrong*.

The modern church is a lot like Arthur Fonzarelli.

We have a hard time saying we're wrong. The rise of rationalism only exasperated the problem. Even if we were wrong, we could argue ourselves into believing it wasn't. Centralized authority—the educated elite—fostered a feeling of rightness. Objective truth was scientifically verifiable. Your truth was your truth, and it was wrong if it wasn't my truth. Since the Reformation, every division in the church is rooted within rationalist theology. "We" (our brand) have a better, more complete, improved idea for how to know God, and if you don't join us, then you're wrong.

In other words, we all put God in our little theological box. Or perhaps, as some antagonists have argued: a coffin.

Consequently, preachers for the past several centuries have centralized and rationalized their messages. Despite Martin Luther's call for a priesthood of all believers to serve as a central theme for reformation, 500 years later we're still far from this ideal. Most Christians will go to a building this Sunday (a box) and enter a room specially designed for a spiritual lecture (a box). They'll sit in their seat (a box) and listen to a single individual pontificate and promote his view of God (a box), as it relates to the church's view of God (a box) and do so behind a lectern or pulpit (a box). The message will be outlined, pointed, and propositional (a box), a persuasive or inspirational argument for God stuff (a box). When the sermon is done (the box emptied), the people will leave their seats and the room (the box emptied) to return to secular spaces. It's no wonder the faith of many believers is compartmentalized.

Sunday is God's time.

The rest of the week is ours.

And yet that frame for this model of "church" is hardly what's revealed for us in the book of Acts. The DNA of the body of Christ was radically different in the first century. Luke outlines it simply in Acts 2:42-47:

> They devoted themselves to the apostles' teaching and to fellowship, to the breaking of bread and to prayer. Everyone was filled with awe at the many wonders and signs performed by the apostles. All the believers were together and had everything in common. They sold property and possessions to give to anyone who had need. Every day they continued to meet together in the temple courts. They broke bread in their homes and ate together with glad and sincere hearts, praising God and enjoying the favor of all the people. And the Lord added to their number daily those who were being saved.

In this passage we discover the *rule* for a Christian worship experience (apostles' teaching, fellowship, breaking of bread[1] and prayer). We also see the *response* of believers (communal sharing, daily fellowship) and the *reaction* of the nonbelieving community (favor, acceptance). The early church met 24/7/365, not 2/1/52. They were dynamic, charismatic, gregarious, and sacrificial. If you were part of the Christian community, you had no need. The church was the ultimate social security and safety net.

I'm going to be brutally honest. This is going to be a hard chapter to read. It's also a difficult chapter to write.

Why?

Because the church has drifted far from this original DNA. We've adopted attractional ("come and see") rather than missional ("go and serve") models. We talk about church as a place ("I went to church yesterday"), when in reality it's the people. We are the church.[2] We are the Temple and New Jerusalem where God dwells. We are the body of Christ. Wherever we go, Jesus goes.

So now for the rub.

We can't teach a church how to be a church—a living organism—if we operate as (and live in) a box. We may inspire a few, but most people will leave unchanged. Plus, let's remember that fewer and fewer Americans are coming to the box. We have to reimagine the Sunday morning event and the primary tool we employ to disciple: a sermon. We have to decentralize our authority and invite everyone into a conversation on spiritual things. It's now time to propose a new wineskin.

THE STARFISH AND THE SPIDER

Ori Brafman and Rod Beckstrom penned a provocative book in 2006 titled *The Starfish and the Spider: The Unstoppable Power of Leaderless Organizations*. The authors proposed a metaphor comparison of starfish and spider, two organisms that look similar but are radically different. A spider is crippled when it's legs are cut off and killed when its head is removed. On the other hand, when a starfish loses a leg, it grows back. Some species of starfish can be cut into several pieces and each part will resurrect a whole new starfish!

You can see starfish organizations all around. They exist as terrorist groups such as Hamas or Al Qaeda or political movements like the Tea Party or Occupy. Most recovery groups and ministries are starfish in nature. Social networking sites like Facebook, YouTube, and Wikipedia operate, according to Brafman and Beckstrom, as "leaderless."

The leadership that does emerge from time to time happens when starfish organizations empower the whole not just the part. In reality, starfish organizations are leader-FULL not leader-less. Every person plays a part. In the natural world, starfish are biologically decentralized so the power and intelligence runs throughout the organism. In contrast, spiders are centralized in nature. Their power and intelligence is confined to the head.

They may look similar with the naked eye, but they are radically different.

Most of us understand spider organizations because that's been the predominant model for centuries. Centralized authority (CEO, lead pastor, general) ruled the day. Centralized systems (flow charts, job descriptions, lines of authority) controlled the organization. Centralized communication (lectures, sermons, orders) kept everyone informed and in line. Everything flowed from the top and the middle like one big volcano. Spider organizations are easily mechanized. Parts are interchangeable and disposable. Intelligence is confined to the highest ranks.

But that world is largely gone.

The world is now flat.

As I've argued, the world's been decentralized by Web and wireless technology. Those generations growing up cyber and digital are allergic to centralized systems, industrial processes, and spider procedures. Many fraternal clubs are dying (too many rules), while communities (social media) are thriving. Before the Internet, community was limited to who you could touch. Today, the whole world can be hugged. Time and space have been redefined from a universe to a multiverse.

> "Decentralization has been lying dormant for thousands of years. But the advent of the Internet has unleashed this force...The absence of structure, leadership, and formal organization, once considered a weakness, has become a major asset. Seemingly chaotic groups have challenged and defeated established institutions. The rules of the game have changed."[3]
>
> —Ori Brafman and Rod A. Beckstrom, *The Starfish and the Spider*

That's why I believe Christianity will explode in a postmodern culture, but we'll have to lose our churchianity (centralized wineskin) to experience it.

Communication will have to change from the sage on the stage model to a guide on the side prototype. I'm thoroughly convinced that sermons, thanks to micro-communication like Twitter and short video content on YouTube, will force increasing brevity. The days are certainly gone when a preacher could hold audiences for hours, days, and even weeks. It's safe to say the traditional sermon of 30 to 45 minutes will probably devolve quickly into a brief 10 to 13 minute homily at best. As the baby boomer generation (the last modern generation) fades into history, don't expect Generation X and millennial communicators to preach as usual. This seems counterintuitive to many church leaders, particularly preachers. A long sermon is traditional. True, but is it practical? Or, more importantly, is it working? The evidence suggests it's not.

THE STARFISH CHURCH

As astute as Brafman and Beckstrom were at identifying historic and current starfish organizations, they missed the greatest one of all: the church.[4] Not the centralized version you and I know, but the decentralized starfish version launched on Pentecost 2,000 years ago. The early church didn't count people; they made people count. They didn't build buildings; they grew a body. They weren't confined to time or space. They met in homes daily. They met in the temple square. They met by riversides, on hills, and anyplace, at any time, they could gather.

The liturgy for this starfish faith community was the apostles' doctrine, fellowship, the Lord's Supper, and prayer (Acts 2:42). Whenever they met as a spiritual community, they invested time in these four elements. We know from other Scriptures and early nonbiblical historical documents that Christians sang psalms, hymns, and other spiritual songs (Ephesians 5:19; Colossians 3:16). In the letter to the Corinthians, we learn the Eucharist, or "Love Feast," was a full meal deal (imitating the multi-course Passover menu). The act of giving was featured in many first-century congregations (2 Corinthians 8:1-3; 9:6-15; Philippians 4:10-19).

The focus of the worship experience was upon community. People sang. People communed. People prayed. People gave.

Church was experiential and interactive.

Just like today's postmodern seeker.

Now to be clear, we can assume there was time in every worship experience for the teaching of the "apostle's doctrine" (which paralleled the teachings of Jesus). We just don't know *how* it happened. In today's church, most people are sermonized with a spiritual lecture. Historically, it's safe to assume that until the Reformation homilies were short (as they remain in Catholic and Orthodox churches to this day). Luther reformed the sermon during his day. He was an academic. Lecture was his primary method. The Enlightenment and Great Awakening gave efficacy to a spiritual lecture as the centerpiece of worship. It was wildly popular and attractive until the advent of television when visual media became a game changer.

The Internet transformed things again, but this time in a more radical way.

Cyber culture is an open system. The power resides in the people. Since the rise of Christendom in A.D. 325, the church has enjoyed a centralized model. Whether pope or priest or preacher, the sermon was one-way, authoritative, and top-down. For centuries, the church (and her communicators) simply shifted within this centralized frame. The modern era merely mechanized it.

But a Web culture has shattered that 1,700-year wineskin. We live in a post-Christendom culture. The world is flat and decentralized. It's left spiders for starfish. And that's why Christianity has a fresh, new edge. We simply need to rediscover our roots, tap into our original DNA, and become the organism we were created to be!

The church in Acts, and the better part of the first three centuries, was decentralized. It had leaders but no leader (save Jesus). It had communicators, but no communicator. There was no single denomination, no single voice, no single curriculum, and no single system. When heresy threatened, the starfish church survived not by control and censorship but by choice and context. The church in

Corinth looked completely different than the church in Jerusalem or Alexandria or Antioch but, nevertheless, maintained by choice the vision and values of Jesus (as learned and relearned through the apostles' teaching).

THE STARFISH SERMON

If you're convinced the world has changed, then you'll probably also agree it's time we fashioned a culturally relevant wineskin for communication in this new world. The sermon method is not sacred. There's no biblical mandate for what it looks like, sounds like, or even feels like. Tradition says, "We've never done it that way before," but those are the seven last words of any church. Actually, tradition is a good thing. It's traditionalism that kills.

Ancient mariners used their anchors for two purposes: to hold fast and to move forward. Many churches anchor their rituals to the past, but when we use traditions to propel us forward that's how we remain relevant and real. What would a starfish sermon look like?

First of all, we need to think in circles not squares.

COME ON, GET LOOPY

If you throw a rock in a lake, it creates circles or loops, each one growing larger as it moves away from the original splash. What if you reimagined your sermons as wave-makers? Your job is to create loops and grow circles of influence.

In the modern world, as mentioned, everything was squared and boxed. We even cut corners. In a starfish culture, loops abound and the only difference is whether you're in or out. Think about Facebook. It's the most basic of all loops. A friend is so loosely defined that you can "friend" someone you've never met!

Prior to the Internet, we lived in a boxed world that barred such loopy behavior.

By nature, Web culture is wet and wild, fast and fluid. It's full of concentric circles. Communication happens all the time via cellular and cyber technology. You may be talking from the stage, but your people, especially the younger postmoderns, are interacting via texts, Facebook, Twitter, and other social media. Pop icon Madonna was booted from a Texas theater for texting during a movie. A particularly clever episode of *The Big Bang Theory* showed how girl-shy Rajesh Koothrappali overcame the obstacle of talking to a new love interest named Lucy (even more socially backward than he) by texting their thoughts…all while standing only feet apart! The difference between the old and new worlds is abundantly evident on a plane. The moment a flight lands, cellphones light up.

But postmoderns communicate by text message while older generations hold verbal conversations (to the dismay of fellow passengers). Texting is more socially acceptable in public space and, in a text culture, to be "all thumbs" is a compliment.

To reimagine your messages as loopy, you need to look at your entire congregation as influencers and partners. Everyone is an equal. Some might have more experience or education or wisdom, but all can contribute something. Perhaps it's a historical insight or a cultural metaphor. Someone might have a slightly different interpretation. Another might possess a powerful application.

If you're in a smaller church, the transition to decentralized loops of influence is rather easy. Communication is already fairly open and fluid. But if you're a pastor of a larger congregation (more than 200 people), this is a more difficult process and requires more intentionality.

Here are a few strategies to move from "me" to "we":

- Announce a week's message topic and Scripture as early as possible. Encourage your people to share stories, links, video clips, illustrations, research, and other helps on your church's Facebook page.

- Invite various artists, videographers, musicians, and thespians in your congregation to create content for the gathering on Sunday and post to Instagram, YouTube, and other social media. Incorporate artistic content into the Sunday experience.

- Instead of asking one person to design the PowerPoint, open it up for any and all interested individuals. This will demand a final outline by Wednesday, but imagine the possibilities. All PowerPoints developed could be available as downloads at the church website.

- During the message, widely advertise your church's Twitter handle (on PowerPoint slides) to encourage individuals to share personal insights and applications. Drive people during your message to the church's Facebook page. Create a buzz or trending topic.

- Use cutting-edge presentation technology like SlideKlowd to instantly interact and know what your audience is thinking.

- Incorporate interactive moments and small group opportunities during the message. Give individuals an opportunity to share with friends what they're discovering from God's Word.

- Invite individuals to relate "popcorn" testimonies. Like "popcorn" prayers (one to three words long), these testimonies release interaction. For example, you might invite people to testify about how God makes them feel during trial.

The secret is not to think outside the box but to imagine there are no boxes at all! We all enjoy loosely defined lines of influence where, once inside, everyone is treated equal. We all have a sermon inside us busting to get out!

MAKING A SPLASH

Every decentralized system has a prominent leader who creates and empowers the circles around stated norms and beliefs. Brafman and Beckstrom referred to this individual as a "catalyst" and astutely cited chemistry to prove their point. After all, the two most common elements in nature are hydrogen and nitrogen. Put them together and nothing happens. However, if you add iron to these two elements, they create ammonia. The irony is there's no iron in ammonia (only hydrogen and nitrogen)!

The catalyst (iron) creates interaction and then disappears.

I believe this will be the primary responsibility of preaching and teaching pastors in the 21st century. In the old modern culture, pastors discipled their congregations to their own strengths (and weaknesses). A church looked like their preacher. This reflection is clearly seen in many larger congregations today. I say "Willowcreek," and you say? I say "Saddleback," and you say? Now both these congregations have done great Kingdom work, but their central leader remains obvious. The test of any congregation is what happens when their beloved pastor departs.

The early church wasn't spiderized. Who was the pastor at Corinth? We know at least three individuals were creating division, Peter, Paul, and Apollos, but none of these men were primary pastors in Corinth (1 Corinthians 1:12), and there's no historical evidence Peter was ever in Corinth! Still, he was an influencer.

> "Once the catalyst leaves, however, his or her presence is still felt. The catalyst is an inspirational figure who spurs others to action."[5]
>
> —Ori Brafman and Rod A. Beckstrom, *The Starfish and the Spider*

You want to starfish your congregation?

Then inspire a loop, interact with and empower the followers, and leave the loop alone.

I'm not saying you leave the church, but rather that you leave your mark on Sunday (at the gathering) and empower the people to pastor and preach the rest of the week in their own circles (home, school, work). You are the guide from the side not the sage from the stage. When your people leave on Sunday morning will they be able to repeat, reproduce, and reinvent your message? Will they *want* to repeat, reproduce, and reinvent your message?

Your sermon must become *their* sermon.

To be an ironclad catalyst that brings a new element to the table, you must start by asking: How can my congregation love and live this teaching? The focus is upon them, not you. Most preachers focus upon their own insights, applications, and ability (centralized spiders), but communicators concentrate on their audience and unleash them (decentralized starfish).

One final thought: What if the missing element for your church's explosive growth (spiritually, numerically, emotionally) is YOU? The nitrogen and hydrogen are just sitting there waiting, but until you interact and dissolve yourself (like Jesus did with his own disciples) to create a new dynamic fusion, nothing will happen. The mystery of God's Kingdom is that less is more, the least are best, and starfish thrive where spiders die.

YOU GOTTA HAVE FAITH

Every starfish organism is saturated with a system of values and beliefs. These are the norms that guide and guard. If these principles mutate, even slightly, eventually division will occur. Some mutations might seem innocuous but are dangerous viruses that cripple and kill. The important part is to remember your roots.

The ostrich egg is one of the earliest symbols of the Coptic Church. Many ancient cathedrals still boast these giant ornate orbs hanging in their midst. But why the ostrich egg? The ostrich is a rather forgetful bird. Its brain is small. When an ostrich deposits her eggs to incubate in the hot sand she can't forget where they are located. Ostriches have the unique ability to see 360 degrees, and their eyes can look in two different directions at the same time.

Consequently, an ostrich mom always keeps one eye on the nest. She never ventures further than eyeshot from the hatch. If she does, she'll forget where she laid her eggs and the whole brood will be lost.

What a powerful Christian symbol! The early churches used ostrich eggs as visual metaphors to never forget the nest. We can look forward but only with one eyeball looking back and staying grounded. Our faith-frame is an anchor. It's more than our creed or theology; it's our philosophy about ministry.

Southwest Airlines is a classic hybrid starfish company. The airline has a CEO but operates rather decentralized. They have no hubs, fly only one type of plane, and every employee is trained (with the exception of flying the plane) to do the work of others. I've seen Southwest pilots cleaning cabins and packing bags. Every employee knows the airline isn't making money when a plane's on the ground. The

Southwest ideology inculcates their company culture: work hard, desire to be the best, innovate, follow the Golden Rule, treat others with respect, put others first, have fun, celebrate successes, be a passionate team player (to name a few).

The number one responsibility for a change-agent is to transfer and translate your church's unique faith-frame to every person, from youngest to oldest. Your ideology will reflect your theological commitments, philosophical foundations, and practical applications. In the modern box church, these were reserved for only a few individuals or leaders. Most people who attend church today cannot share what their church believes or why it does what it does. This will have to change in a flat, fluid culture or else the next generation will forget and be lost.

PLUG IN AND BOOT UP

Every starfish needs to plug in to power up.

In a word, we need to network. We need to use our resources.

Communicators rest upon resources, and power sparks through interaction. Your networks include previous mentors, educators, pastors, leaders, organizations, websites, institutions, and cultural expressions. When you stop to think about it, a great sermon isn't born in a vacuum. It's a collection of scattered bits, bites, and bytes that we've heard, experienced, learned, or discovered by accident over the years. Master communicators possess countless resources and continually process new information and insights.

A personal goal I have for every message is to consult no less than ten sources. These sources can be commentaries, websites, journals, dictionaries, and encyclopedias. But resource ideas also spark in my conversations and connections. I might hear a great tale at my Toastmaster Club or a stirring story on the nightly news. I might draw inspiration from something I see in the natural world or reading a compelling quote on Facebook. I might go to a movie and find an illustration or draw from a personal experience in my past. Your network is wide, but it's only as deep as what you're able to capture through personal experience.

Think of your network as your *net worth*. What's your intellectual capital? How rich is your treasury of truth? How can you invest in learning and expanding your reach? No preacher is an island. And in a wireless Web world, you have it all at your fingertips. Just a call or click away.

WE ARE THE CHAMPIONS

Every organization needs champions. Change-agents are the visionaries. They communicate the faith system. Champions are charismatic leaders who have grasped the vision and advocate the beliefs to current, new, and emerging loops.

Champions are preachers in the wings.

They're watching you. They're learning from you. They're modeling your techniques. You are the change agent, but every change agent needs at least one champion. Without a champion, a movement is confined to a single personality.

Want to create champions in your preaching ministry? Host a sermon community on Mondays and invite various individuals to help you interpret, understand, and apply the passage. Allow emerging champions to share brief devotional thoughts to the Sunday gathering and hone their speaking skills. Start a Toastmaster public speaking club in your church (this will draw speakers and leaders). Slowly turn the preaching reigns over to others. Starfish churches don't boast a single preacher but rather several individuals who speak. You may be one of the preachers, but you're not speaking every Sunday.

Can you imagine a church where every person has the potential and opportunity to preach? It doesn't mean everyone will (or should). Remember, the circles drawn can be very exclusive. I believe those who lead and speak on a Sunday morning should be an elite group, the best of the best. But that doesn't mean others can't talk, share, confess, testify, inspire, apply, and communicate.

Postmoderns are wildly attracted to spiritual experiences that flatten hierarchy and fluidly communicate. The world has changed. The wine remains the same, but the wineskins are now leaking like a sieve. We must reimagine an interactive, experiential, image-soaked wineskin that effectively communicates truth to a postmodern culture. Sticking our head in the sand will only cost us the next generation. The future is in the water.

Starfish thrive in a wet Web world, while spiders will drown.

Even the Fonz had to eventually learn to water ski.

Endnotes

1. The "breaking of bread" was an early reference to the Eucharist, or Lord's Supper. While fellowship was often meal events that had moments of "breaking of bread," the use of it in connection to worship was clearly a Communion experience, especially on the first day (Sunday) when the church gathered to remember the Resurrection (Acts 20:7; 1 Corinthians 10:16).

2. A church is not a place but a people (Matthew 18:17; Acts 5:11; 8:3; 11:26; 12:15; 14:27; 15:3, 22, 30; 1 Corinthians 11:18; 14:23). On several occasions the Apostle Paul says to greet the "church" that meets in a house (Romans 16:5; 1 Corinthians 16:19, Colossians 4:15; Philemon 1:2). The house isn't called a church, the people are.

3. Ori Brafman and Rod A. Beckstrom, *The Starfish and the Spider: The Unstoppable Power of Leaderless Organizations* (New York, NY: Penguin Group, 2006), 6-7.

4. It's fair to argue that God's intent for his people is "starfish," or decentralized in nature. In the Old Testament, multiple leaders led the community of God at any one time (judges, prophets). It wasn't until the people demanded a king in Samuel's day that Israel centralized and made Jerusalem its focus city (eventually building a temple to house God). This spiderfication of the Israelites would seed their doom. Within a few centuries, they were overthrown by Assyria and Babylon.

5. Ori Brafman and Rod A. Beckstrom, *The Starfish and the Spider: The Unstoppable Power of Leaderless Organizations* (New York, NY: Penguin Group, 2006), 93.

Chapter Six:
THE TRUTH IS OUT THERE

"We don't yet see things clearly. We're squinting in a fog, peering through a mist. But it won't be long before the weather clears and the sun shines bright! We'll see it all then, see it all as clearly as God sees us, knowing him directly just as he knows us!"
—1 Corinthians 13:12, *The Message*

"I still haven't found what I'm looking for."[1]
—U2

I do my best thinking on the back of a motorcycle.

I suspect it's because it gets me outside the box or the "cage" (aka a car) and allows me to journey to God knows where.

No one wants to ride a motorcycle in a straight line. Curves are more fun (and dangerous). On a sun-drenched day, many a biker will take the long way home, get off the beaten path, or follow their nose and the wind. I've actually discovered some new eating haunts riding my Harley, not just in the spirit of exploration, but because I could smell the food cooking. When you ride a motorbike, you experience everything. You taste the air (and occasional bug), feel the temperature changes, smell the distinct odors, hear the roar of the pipes, and see stuff missed when rolling down the road in a temperature-controlled cage.

The experience unleashes countless insights, ideas, and imaginations.

I've also learned the greatest difference between riding a motorcycle and driving a car is the *doubt*. I really don't know when I'll get home. Even as an experienced biker, I still doubt my skills, and so I'm more aware when turning, accelerating, or stopping. I doubt every driver around me. I want them to know I'm there. I give plenty of space. I constantly scan for potential lane changes. And if you're talking on a cellphone I'm going to pass you when safe. To be honest, I don't think as much when I drive a car. I zone out more. I listen to talk radio. I control the environment.

And I miss a lot of the journey.

Most of us drive a car to get somewhere as fast (and safe) as possible. For a biker, the purpose of the ride is the journey (with all the risks involved). Every moment counts.

I'm convinced if we're going to attract and engage postmoderns, we'll need to get out of our philosophical and theological cages to embrace and experience the journey. For hundreds of years modern culture operated within the box. Truth was mechanized and reduced to three criteria: certainty, objectivity, and goodness.[2] Learning was linear and focused upon right answers. Communication happened within a controlled-environment.

But now imagine a world where everyone under 55 is riding a motorcycle and those under 30 have *never* even been in a car! Every year there are fewer cars on the road. The caged driving experience is going the way of the dinosaur because nobody buys a car anymore. The postmodern generations ride to be free and to experience the journey. Why would anyone trap himself or herself inside a car and miss the moment? Life is more than getting someplace. It's enjoying the ride.

I think this metaphor attacks a fundamental problem with preaching today: its propositional nature. For hundreds of years an Enlightenment culture thrived on propositional truth and strategies. Modern culture wanted things to make sense. Nonsense was devilish, childish, and foolish. In an age of science, truth was ordered, classified, and reduced to hypothesis and testing. The truth was out there, and we could understand it. Consequently, preaching in the modern era was propositional. Every homiletic student learned how to write a thesis statement and propose proofs, solutions, or reasons. We got a lot of mileage out of particular makes and models, most notably expository preaching.

But that car culture has run out of gas.

In a car, only one person has the wheel and everyone else travels where the driver takes him or her. In the emerging biker culture, every person has his or her own wheels. You don't need a chauffeur. Nor do you want to take a taxi for truth. The truth is out there. Don't take me; show me. Don't tell me; point me in the direction. Don't trap me within your cage of what you know (Google can tell me that!). Fill my tank with insight and inspiration, and then let me go experience Christ.

> "The sermon itself usually concentrates on drawing out some truth from one or more Bible passages. It takes the form of a lecture: the speaker talks for twenty minutes or so, without interruption, showing his audience the truths that the Bible contains. The congregation listens passively for the most part, though some people may take notes. The goal is the transmission of knowledge."[3]
>
> —Heath White, *Postmodernism 101*

If you're an older preacher, it's completely counter to what you were taught and practiced for years. I know. I learned the same strategies and still have trouble breaking free of the idea that my car is the only vehicle that can make the trip.

I DOUBT IT

The patron saint of postmodern culture is Thomas.

But I think this doubting disciple gets a bad rap. Thomas didn't doubt Jesus as much as his own experience *with* Jesus. Unlike the other disciples, Thomas had only heard of Jesus' resurrection. For whatever reason, Thomas was AWOL when Jesus made his initial public appearance to the disciples. Thomas simply wanted to experience Jesus just like his friends. He wanted to feel Jesus personally to confirm the buzz.

You see, there are two types of doubt. First, there is negative doubt that paralyzes and produces instability. James writes about this type of doubt:

> "In the postmodern world, people are no longer convinced that knowledge is inherently good. In eschewing the Enlightenment myth of inevitable progress, postmodernism replaces the optimism of the last century with a gnawing pessimism."[4]
>
> —Stanley Grenz, *A Primer on Postmodernism*

> *If any of you lacks wisdom, you should ask God, who gives generously to all without finding fault, and it will be given to you.* ***But when you ask, you must believe and not doubt, because the one who doubts is like a wave of the sea, blown and tossed by the wind.*** *That person should not expect to receive anything from the Lord. Such a person is double-minded and unstable in all they do.* (James 1:5-8)

Doubt that paralyzes faith and shutters belief cannot grow faith or inspire wisdom. A wavering opinion is spiritual schizophrenia.

On the other hand, positive doubt produces learning. All learning originates within doubt and ignorance. We don't know that we don't know, and then we know what we didn't know that we didn't know (you got that?). Thomas was a disciple (or learner) of Christ. Jesus taught Thomas to critically think for himself, and he wasn't about to deny previous learning experiences.

After all, it was Thomas who charged the other disciples to return to hostile Judea for Lazarus's funeral, even if it meant death (John 11:16). Thomas also queried Jesus about how to follow him, only to learn his Master was the way, the truth, and the life (John 14:5-6). Thomas' doubt didn't paralyze him. He wasn't unstable in his opinions about Jesus. Thomas was a learner, and every disciple seeks understanding from a point of doubt. So when Jesus shows up a second time to his disciples, he fingers Thomas's doubt (John 20:26-28): *Touch me. You're real. The wounds are real. I'm real. This whole thing is real.*

Postmoderns seek *reality*. In a digital world where images and documents can be manipulated, reality gets distorted. Virtual reality alters truth. What looks real isn't. Video games feel real, but they're not. Consequently, younger generations hunger to touch Truth. In the modern world, we said, *"I'll believe it when I see it."* But in a postmodern culture we say, *"I'll believe it when I experience it."* The Way of Truth to touch Life is a journey not a destination. Doubt is the fuel that sparks a relentless pursuit of what's truly real.

> "Welcome to the real world."[5]
> —Morpheus to Neo, *The Matrix*

GOOGLING GOD

Postmoderns Google answers. Google is a verb. That phrase is so hard that even my grammar and spell check won't let me write it. It doesn't make sense, but we all know it's true (unless you're one of the remaining Luddites on the planet who hasn't posted a query to Google).

In a modern world, mechanized to pour truth into nuggets (boxes), the communicator was the expert and manipulated, organized, and censored what was learned. He or she had more schooling, richer experiences, greater resources, and better relationships with people who knew the answers. The school and church—the two great learning institutions of the past 500 years—operated like a machine. Students were matriculated along a curriculum path. Every learner was treated the same, and those who couldn't keep up were politely rerouted to "alternative" forms of education.

The point of modern education was to eliminate questions. The more you knew, the fewer questions you possessed. Of course, that's a myth. Any truly learned person would confess they are *consciously* ignorant. Most people are *unconsciously* ignorant. They don't know what they don't know. They don't even know what questions to ask (without feeling stupid). Maybe that's why Google is popular. A search engine levels no critique of the question or questioner.

At our human core we are naturally curious. We are born not with a silver spoon in our mouth but a question on our lips.

Preschoolers burst with marvel. *How does this work? Why is this happening? Where does this go? What happens when I do this? When will we get there?* But they get the questions educated out of them. By the time these tykes graduate high school, the questions have disappeared (replaced with GPAs, test scores, and a diploma). In four years of college, professors will continue the content dumps. The only question on these minds full of facts: *Is this going to be on the test?*

Modern education (including Christian) snuffed the questions and taught to the test. Doubt was wrong. The professor (or preacher) was always right. After all, he or she had the education, experiences, resources, and connections. Who was I to argue with someone who claimed to have all the answers?

Then Google came along and changed the rules. A whole new world opened up where questions were welcomed and the answers were many.

The Internet flattened intellectual hierarchies and equalized knowledge. The answers were no longer confined to a book or teacher but scattered throughout the multiverse of a cyber sea. And search engines like Google floated the best solutions our way. In a 30-minute Google search, a student learns more about a subject than four years of lectures. We now have full access to resources. Many former students ask me questions via Facebook or email. In the old modern world, such luxury was lost after graduation. The professor was no longer needed. Today, learning is lifelong and a teacher simply lengthens his or her class roster.

For preaching to be effective, we'll have to embrace doubt. Skepticism is part of the journey. Questioning is welcomed. In the New International Version of the Bible, there are 57 times in the Old and New Testament where the word (or a derivative) "question" appears. Half of these (28) are directly tied to Jesus. Jesus was a master at drawing out questions. People queried him often. This was not an uncommon learning strategy of his day. Rabbis, gurus, and other teachers routinely taught through questions and nearly always produced more questions. In Luke 2:46, Jesus is found in the Temple listening to the rabbis and asking them questions. Some of Jesus' best-loved stories emerged through questioning.[6] Jesus' disciples sometimes pulled him aside to further explain a parable (Matthew 13:36).

The seed to every question is doubt. We don't know and must inquire to learn. Master teachers and communicators don't give answers but spark more questions. They wear the learner out, filling their mind with curiosity rather than cramming it full of facts. This was actually the standard in education until the rise of the university in the Middle Ages. The Enlightenment married the Industrial Revolution to birth the educational beast we witness today: 12 grade levels plus post-secondary and graduate levels that run like clockwork along an assembly line. Each grade level steals a few more questions and attaches more knowledge like parts on a car.

This system was efficacious because it could be controlled. The classroom and church hall were under the watch of a single influencer (who was monitored by higher controls like school districts and denominational headquarters). The answers were given as needed. Student and congregation were introduced to knowledge systematically and sequentially. And it all happened within specified time and space.

Not so today.

With the click of a mouse or the swipe of a finger, anyone can be anywhere learning anything at anytime. I Googled "Google" and received 15,430,000,000 results in .53 seconds! Then I Googled "God" and it returned 2,450,000,000 in .58 seconds. What does it say when Google beats God both in sheer number and speed? Google started in 1998 with 3.6 million searches (9,800 per day). In 2013, there were 2.1 trillion searches, or 5.9 billion per day![7] The population of the planet is 7 billion and growing.[8] Google has nearly as many searches in one day as our globe has people.

That's why it's foolish to think one-way communication and centralized intellectual capitals will still work in a Web world. Modernity was hinged by CONTROL. In postmodern culture we are wired by CHOICE. We want options. We hunger for a personalized experience. We detest one size fits all clothing, technology, and answers.

And what ultimately fuels a choice culture?

Doubt.

Don't believe me? The hottest business in the past five years has been self-styled eateries. Have you gone out for yogurt lately? Now you pay by the pound. No longer does someone make your sweet treat. You build it yourself and add your own candies, syrups, and toppings. With all the options, we can't have it all. Consequently, doubt drives our choices and produces some funky new flavors. If you have satellite television you know the hundreds of channels create doubt. What's more frustrating than scores of networks and still nothing to watch? Doubt drives us to keep searching.

TRUTH DECAY

Pilate once asked Jesus the million-dollar question: "What is truth?" (John 18:38). The ageless inquiry was compartmentalized for most of the modern era inside tidy theological and philosophical packages. For most of human history, truth has been centralized and flowed through respected, trusted sources (whether parent or teacher or clergy). During modernity, the mechanization of truth created entire denominations, organizations, schools, and political parties committed to protect the view and insure truth wasn't watered down. The philosophical emergence of objective truth during the Enlightenment further framed certainty.

> "The question is no longer 'Is it true?' but 'What use is it?'"[9]
>
> —Stanley Grenz,
> *A Primer on Postmodernism*

For the modern, objectivity created security and a host of "isms." Rationalism. Pragmatism. Realism. Humanism. Darwinism. Creationism. Communism.

Socialism. Fascism. Racism. Fundamentalism. Liberalism. Dogmatism. Atheism. Agnosticism. You can't spell "schism" without "ism." Modernity was about confining truth to a box.

But what happens when a truth frame is shattered? Actually, there are only two options: Choose the new truth box (change positions) or grow agnostic (embrace doubt). During modernity, it's no surprise that rhetoric, argument, and logic were popular devices to persuade someone outside our box. The debate was won by whoever proved more convincing, whether in word, deed, pen, film, or song.

For the modern, doubt was weakness. It was better to be an atheist (with a firm position) than an agnostic. But that's also no longer true. In fact, the narrower the frame, the less persuasive a view becomes. In a choice culture, truth is varied and agnosticism a virtue. The postmodern argues

> "No one has access to all reality in such a way that can conclusively call his experience and understanding the truth...We benefit when we are in contact with others who help us develop new categories...This is how we grow, learn, and develop."[10]
>
> —Doug Pagitt, *Preaching Re-Imagined*

that "I may not know everything, but at least I embrace doubt and confess my skepticism." Ultimately that's far more persuasive than someone who claims to possess an exclusive, pure, and absolute brand of truth.

Many people who come to church today are Christian agnostics. Oh yes, they believe in Jesus, but when pressed to confess, they don't know why or how they believe. Most postmoderns I meet, including Christians, are *theo-nostic*. They believe in God but embrace, even enjoy, doubt and eclecticism in their spiritual journeys. They affirm Jesus but question the boxes constructed by parents, preachers, professors, and peers. It's not enough to know God. Postmoderns want to touch him. They want to feel the Divine, and they'll pick and choose to build a God that suits and satisfies.

The greatest validation of truth is personal experience.

Consequently, the postmodern is allergic to objective truth because it's just a frame of interpretation. It's what someone claims to be true. It's what a person says is right. But how do we truly know that we know? Objective truth is a modern myth. Absolute truth resembles sunlight. It's out there. But what color is it? All colors? No color? Yellow? White? And yet a prism refracts the light into a kaleidoscope of colors. This is how the postmodern views truth. Few deny that absolute truth exists (just like sunlight exists) but rather contend truth is revealed through the prism of individual perspectives (or experience) and is, by consequence, rather relative.

The modern took their color of choice in the prism, objectified, and even deified it. If your truth was blue, then pity, fight, or belittle the yellows and reds. Modern denominations (emerging in the past 500 years) are merely theological colors objectified into creeds. Postmoderns believe objectivity is an illusion. That's why you'll hear them quip, "Your truth is *your* truth. This is *my* truth." We all embrace our own personal truths. Human truth is relative and subjective.

MY STORY, YOUR STORY, HIS STORY, OUR STORY

When you look out at your congregation this Sunday, do you see a crowd with a story or untold stories within the crowd? There is a difference. Preaching in a fluid culture recognizes no one enjoys the same life journey. Consequently, we all possess a personal (subjective) truth that's emerged from our experiences and education, culture and context. That's why lectures and monologues without interaction fall upon deaf ears and so easily bore. Postmoderns are skeptical of boxes and bristle at anyone who claims to speak *for* God. Maybe God is on your side, but unless we journey together (in conversation), I don't know for sure.

> "I had to be 'depropositionalized.' Rather than seeing the gospel as propositions, mechanisms, abstractions or universal concepts, I came to see the gospel as a narrative, a story, a 'once there was a man named Joseph engaged to a woman named Mary' type of account."[11]
>
> —Brian D. McLaren, *The Church in Emerging Culture*

Paul understood the fragility of human truth and how we all live a story within the Story. Paul says we are living "letters" (2 Corinthians 3:3). In other words, there's the Old Testament, the New Testament, and the Me Testament. My life is part of HIS story. It's HIStorical. Paul also recognized that no one has a corner on absolute truth, for we all gaze through glass that's darkened, damaged, and dull. We only know in part, but someday all will be clear (1 Corinthians 13:12).[12]

Consequently, narrative preaching strategies are powerful and persuasive. Wikipedia refers to narrative preaching as the "New Homiletic" and explains it thus:

> *The New Homiletic is a reaction against propositional preaching. It requires the preacher to take an expectant, imaginative stance before the biblical text. The goal of the sermon is a transformative event, often requiring a strategic delay of meaning. In other words, the preacher does not give the congregation the thesis or point at the beginning of the sermon; they are required to follow along as the preacher explores the text and its meaning. Language is used carefully to produce the desired effect; what language does is considered more important than what it says. Poetic and metaphorical language is privileged. Stories and metaphors are points; they do not illustrate them.*

The sermon is structured in such a way that an early imbalance or disconnect leads to some sort of resolution by the end of the sermon; a story is not required. Stories function as the structure and logic of the sermon, not necessarily its content.[13]

In other words, we journey with our audience to a destination. The points are not the point. In fact, if your points don't point to the Point (Jesus), your preaching is pointless.

Narratives are a popular cultural technique in television and movies, and they are easily seen in a comparison between *The Brady Bunch* and *Modern Family*. The formula for the sitcom has changed. Originally, a half-hour comedy presented a situation (hence the name: sitcom). For example, Bob, Carol, and the "bunch" began with a problem around a particular character (like Cindy's lisp or Greg's hair) and resolved it. Each episode stood alone. Next week there was a new "situation." Today's sitcoms are more fluid. Storylines last all season, even multiple seasons. Each episode moves to a point of resolution while the stories and characters continue to unfold.

A lot of preaching today is expository. This form of preaching dissects (exposes) passages of Scripture then neatly explains and applies the truths discovered. Each week's sermon is mostly disconnected from the previous. Every week a new passage is framed and exposed, often with little to no connective transitions. Consequently, the overall Story can be lost, forgotten, or missed.

I was trained in expository preaching, and I love verse-by-verse dissections, but I have long struggled with any method that reduces Scripture to a science experiment. How many modern pulpiteers in the name of systematic theology have caused biblical injustices, even abuse? The Word of God is living and active. It's a dangerously sharp Sword. But it's also the Greatest Story Rarely Told. How many sermons are heard on Noah, Numbers, or Nebuchadnezzar? Not many. The reason is these biblical episodes don't fit nor preach well (as expository messages). Noah is better left to the little ones. Numbers is ancient history. And Nebuchadnezzar just isn't important. And yet God still included them in his story. They are stories within the Story.

Narratives draw an audience into the cultural context and the lives of the characters. So an incident like the woman caught in adultery (John 8) is less about three things we can learn (propositions) and more about why she committed this sin, how Jesus responded, and what it meant to her. Narrative preaching reveals the story behind the story.

But let me clear. Narrative preaching is part of the process. To be powerful and personal, however, we must add substantial interaction. It's essential to personally involve people within the biblical story. As preachers, to be effective with emerging generations we must also guide conversations about the selected text. Our part is minimal. We answer a question (briefly). We inspire insight or ideas through a video clip, personal story, or experiential activity. We share a helpful resource.

> One of my favorite preaching passages is Hebrews 11, or the "Hall of Faith" chapter. In this chapter we learn about Old Testament heroes like Abel, Enoch, Noah, Abraham, Isaac, Jacob, Joseph, Moses, Rahab, Gideon, Barak, Samson, Jephthah, David, and Samuel. If you're a good Bible student, you've recognized most of these names…but did a couple names catch you off guard? I bet one did. Ever hear a sermon on Jephthah? Take a moment and read Judges 11. See how easy it is to miss a great story?

The goal of conversational narrative preaching can be found in the words of John the Baptist: "He must become greater, I must become less" (John 3:30). Our role is to point people to Christ. Like John the Baptist, we are a voice crying in the wilderness that reveals the Messiah. It's not about us. It's not about what we know. It's not about our profound words or penetrating insights or powerful applications.

We are not the source of information as much as a resource. We are not the sun but the moon. We reflect, deflect, and inflect.

How do we become *less*?

Simple. We release the conversation to the people. In a 40-minute sermon, there's no reason the congregation couldn't use half that time to connect, interact, share, debate, defend, explain, outline, persuade, and propose. That still leaves 20 minutes for you to communicate what you've learned on the passage.

DECONSTRUCTING

My mentor Dr. Leonard Sweet once quipped, "In order to understand a person we must learn to stand under them." Essentially, we cannot know another individual until we've walked their journey, preferably wearing their shoes, and experienced as much as possible their life.

Postmodern philosophers identified this process as deconstruction. From the stories and experiences of a person we learn who they are, why they behave how they do, how they think, and where they've been.

Similarly, before we can preach a passage, we comprehend it by walking with it. But this means far more than commentary work, Greek study, or cultural research. Jacques Derrida promoted "deconstructionism" and argued there is no meaning outside the text. In other words, no text stands alone when we read and interpret it. Rather it's guided by countless readings and interpretations of the text that stretch from the moment it was penned to this very day.

> "The pastor's preaching indicates a serious engagement with the early fathers and the Reformers as co-interpreters. All of this helps us understand that the church is a community, a 'holy, catholic church,' which has endured through millennia."[14]
>
> —James K.A. Smith, *Who's Afraid of Postmodernism?*

Therefore, our interpretation is only as strong as our journey with the text. We can learn how early church fathers interpreted it. We can also interact with previous messages we've heard, historical essays, Christian music, insights from peers, class notes, experiences, Web searches, and countless other influences.

Modern propositional, expository preaching proposed solutions, frames, and orthodoxy (right thinking). In contrast, postmodern narrative, interactive preaching will offer stories, lens, and orthopraxy (right behavior). Truth no longer comes in a box. Rather, it's eyewear (think Google Glasses). We help our congregation discover the Truth—through stories—in order to have improved vision about the past, present, and future. We guide and guard, lead and load, reveal and revise. We journey with people to connect their personal truths to the absolute truth of Jesus Christ. Jesus was the Word and the Word became flesh (John 1:14). Jesus is not a word or words. He cannot be confined by a statement or sentence. Nor can he be packaged within proposition or proposal. Jesus incarnated as fully human. Do we even dare reduce his story into clever argument and nifty packaging? And yet many do.

When we embrace Christ as flesh and Scripture as living and active, we lift up a message that attracts postmoderns.

THE RIDE HOME

In late summer 2003, hundreds of thousands of Harley-Davidson bikers committed to the "ride home" in honor of a century of Harley manufacturing. Motorcyclists chose from four points (Las Vegas, Portland, Baton Rouge, and New York City) to make the ride to Milwaukee, the home of Harley-Davidson. The ride was free and open to the public. Along the way there were festivals, special events, and other motorcycle activities.

Harley bikers joined the rally locally and could ride as far as they desired. Many rode all the way "home" to Milwaukee. The thunder of thousands of Harleys rolling over plains, through towns and cities, across summits, and along valley floors was a special, historic experience. It's the same feelings that still annually motivate bikers to congregate in Daytona, Laconia, Laughlin, and Sturgis. Bikers are family. Yes, there are the one-percenters (hard core, violent bikers), but most motorcyclists are down home, salt of the earth, everyday Joes and Janes.

The first time I wrapped my legs around the iron horse, revved the engine, and jetted down a lonely road, I was hooked. My mind was free, and every mile proved a memory. I get judged by a lot of non-bikers for my dangerous pastime, but that's okay. Riding a hog has made me a better man, and I could pursue worse vices. Besides, until you've ridden a thousand miles on a bike, you wouldn't understand (and I'm fine with that truth).

We all make a ride home.

Life is about the journey into eternity. Many will choose to cruise through their lives in a cage, trapped by choices. Inside the cage there's an undeniable comfort zone and ease. It's possible to snooze and speed through life, missing what's truly important, or to get stuck, stranded, or sideswiped by circumstance and crisis.

Maybe that's why the wise still wrap their spiritual legs around something different. They get out of the cage and experience every sound, sight, and smell. They ride for the journey not the destination. It's clearly a postmodern value.

Our work as preachers is to call people out of their comfort zones and caged existence. And the best strategy is to season the journey with doubt. Free people to enjoy the ride and live the life. We can't order our days or schedule our lives completely. Stuff happens along the road to detour and delay. A great ride is seasoned with rich conversation. There's joy in the JOurneY, if you look.

In the end, all we really leave in our legacy is a story.

Our story *and* His story.

Endnotes

1. U2, "I Still Haven't Found What I'm Looking For," *The Joshua Tree* (album), 1987.

2. Stanley Grenz wrote, "The pursuit of dispassionate knowledge divides the scientific project into separate disciplines…In addition to assuming knowledge is certain and objective, Enlightenment thinkers also assume it is inherently good… [which] renders the Enlightenment outlook optimistic." Stanley Grenz, *A Primer on Postmodernism* (Grand Rapids, MI: William B. Eerdmans Publishing, 1996), 4.

3. Heath White, *Postmodernism 101* (Grand Rapids, MI: Brazos Press, 2006), 35.

4. Stanley Grenz, *A Primer on Postmodernism*, (Grand Rapids, MI: William B. Eerdmans Publishing, 1996), 7.

5. International Movie Database, *The Matrix*, "Quotes," http://www.imdb.com/title/tt0133093/trivia?tab=qt&ref_=tt_trv_qu.

6. In Luke 10:25-37, Jesus tells the story of the good Samaritan. During this exchange, four questions are asked, two by a lawyer and two by Jesus: "What must I do to inherit eternal life" and "who is my neighbor?" (lawyer) and "How do you read it?" and "Which of these three do you think was a neighbor to the man who fell into the hands of robbers?"

7. "Google Annual Search Statistics," Statistic Brain, http://www.statisticbrain.com/google-searches/.

8. Watch our world population grow: http://www.worldometers.info/world-population/.

9. Stanley Grenz, *A Primer on Postmodernism*, (Grand Rapids, MI: William B. Eerdmans Publishing, 1996), 48.

10. Doug Pagitt, *Preaching Re-Imagined*, (Grand Rapids, MI: Zondervan, 2005), 136-137.

11. Leonard Sweet (ed.), Andy Crouch, Michael Horton, Frederica Mathewes-Green, Brian D. McLaren, Erwin McManus, *The Church in Emerging Culture*, (Grand Rapids, MI: Zondervan, 2003), 198.

12. In Acts 17, Paul preaches to the Athenians and notes their religious diversity, including how they've erected an idol to an "unknown god." Paul doesn't condemn their idolatry but rather uses the idol as a bridge to Jesus Christ. Jesus is the one they don't know (yet). For these Athenians, religious truth was very relative and personal. Paul wasn't afraid to enter that world to point people to Christ.

13. "Narrative Preaching," *Wikipedia, The Free Encyclopedia,* http://en.wikipedia.org/wiki/Narrative_preaching.

14. James K. A. Smith, *Who's Afraid of Postmodernism?* (Grand Rapids, MI: Baker Academic, 2006), 57.

Chapter Seven:
FEED THE NEED

"Jesus went through all the towns and villages, teaching in their synagogues, proclaiming the good news of the kingdom and healing every disease and sickness. When he saw the crowds, he had compassion on them, because they were harassed and helpless, like sheep without a shepherd."

—Matthew 9:35-36

"Everybody's got a hungry heart."[1]

—Bruce Springsteen

Naked and afraid.

It's a compelling yet controversial reality show on the Discovery Channel. The premise is simple: Two strangers are left alone to survive for 21 days in some of the planet's most brutal and dangerous climates. From the Amazon jungle to the Serengeti to a remote Fiji island, a man and woman must survive three weeks with a single survival tool of choice (most favor either a fire starter or knife).

No water. No food. No shelter. And no clothes.

This final component is the most challenging hurdle, not just in social interaction but also in pure survival. The absence of clothing presents an entirely new degree of difficulty. What you wear is your final defense against weather, critters, and injury. Without shoes, walking becomes a peril. Without shirt and pants, the sun becomes a dangerous adversary. Without clothes, there is no buffer or barrier from stinging insects, poisonous plants, and infectious diseases.

Many of the players tap out after several days. Some are hospitalized for a variety of injuries or diseases. All face down some of their greatest fears.

Now you know why the show is called *Naked and Afraid*.

In their three-week journey, the survivalists must work together to build shelter, forage food, and tap safe water. In the process they'll lose 15 to 30 pounds and become a shell of their former self. If the natural elements, including vicious heat and dangerous storms, aren't furious enough, the social game is a true nemesis. Participants also receive no compensation. The only reward is pushing your body in an extreme climate and surviving both the elements and each other.

Once the initial awkwardness of nudity is overcome, the real test is how do two complete strangers interact without killing each other? You can't tell me cannibalism doesn't cross the mind of a starving, frustrated castaway! When you're willing to eat bark and feed on flowers, the yapping of an obnoxious partner might prove the last (delicious) straw.

Naked and afraid.

It's a hit reality show for the couch potato survivalist. It's also how Jesus regarded his congregation. According to one of his biographers, Jesus viewed people as helpless and harassed (Matthew 9:36). Sheep without a shepherd. Sick and diseased. Naked and afraid. But don't miss the bigger point. Not only did Jesus understand their context, he felt it personally. He had compassion for them. Jesus sensed their pain. The Greek is even more helpful. The word for compassion is *splanchnizomai* and literally means "to feel it in the gut." When Jesus saw his culture, his stomach hurt. His congregation caused him to ache on the inside.

When you craft a message, do you feel their pain? *You should.*

When you look into their eyes, do you view their angst? *You need to.*

Do you preach until it hurts? *You'd better.*

One of the grand paradigm shifts for the postmodern communicator is to focus not upon a selected text but rather upon the audience and their contexts. Sunday after Sunday, the people gather naked and afraid. Some are financially or professionally stripped and fear their futures. Others have been disrobed by hidden sin and live with shame and guilt. Still others are emotionally exposed and rubbed raw from circumstances, crises, and conflicts. Many will come friendless, feeling worthless and insecure. Others will arrive at church psychologically naked: crippled by anger and angst, wounded by pride and prejudice, and scarred by abuse and addiction.

So what do people need? I can tell you what they don't need.

They don't need a sermon. They don't need another lecture on how life hurts. They don't need to feel guilty for their faults and failures. They're already naked and afraid. Helpless and harassed. Hurt and hopeless.

A primary purpose of the Protestant sermon for the past 500 years was indoctrination. It was aimed at the head to eliminate ignorance, eradicate doubt, and empower objectivity. Truth was something to be grasped. Consequently, the

> "Do not let any unwholesome talk come out of your mouths, but only what is helpful for building others up **according to their needs**, that it may benefit those who listen."
>
> —Ephesians 4:29

modern preacher crafted sermons to inform, persuade, and defend. The congregation marched like soldiers under command. If you had problems, put on your camouflage. Gas mask your insecurity. Protect your hypocrisy with soul armor. Cloak your doubts with weapons of mass instruction. The modern mind hungered for answers, so preachers operated like ecclesiastical Pez dispensers doling out candy-coated clarifications. Don't misunderstand; that's not a bad thing, and it was a highly effective strategy in an Enlightenment era.

It just no longer works.

The postmodern generation embraces doubt, risk, transparency, and journey. Life isn't about answers but questions. Postmoderns crave safe communities where conversation happens. Why? Because interaction breeds understanding and comprehension grows conviction. In a Google world, answers are everywhere, so there's no need to go to a church building to listen to one man's solutions. Postmoderns fear ignorance and resent one-size-fits-all resolutions. The first sign of a cult is someone with all the answers.

Some futurists predict the church of tomorrow will naturally become smaller. Span of control limits a leader to eight people. Jesus worked with twelve. The larger the crowd, the less conversation happens. The megachurch movement turned the Sunday service into a staged presentation event. But in a coffee shop world where Google answers every question, the characteristics of postmodern spiritual experiences will be interaction, experiential learning, and imagery. It won't be enough to hold attention if you can't hold a conversation. It won't matter if you speak well if you can't craft captivating metaphors and design engaging experiences. And, without a doubt, the secret sauce to success will be size. It's easy to chat in a Honda Civic but far more difficult to guide conversations in a Greyhound bus.

Does that mean events and large churches are history? Not necessarily. But worship and teaching were never meant to be an event. Whenever Jesus attracted a crowd of thousands, the opportunity to teach devolved into a miracle event (Matthew 14:13-21; 15:29-39). In fact, the last time Jesus drew a crowd of thousands, he didn't teach at all. He just performed miracles (Mark 8:1-10). Outside of Pentecost, the first-century church operated mostly in small spaces (homes, courtyards, river banks) with a handful of people. The modern church, particularly in the latter half of the 20th century, focused on numbers to produce events (revivals, services, conferences, retreats). Preaching proved particularly efficient once the voice could be artificially amplified, first by cathedral acoustics and then by electronic microphones.[2]

The industrialization of the church was about efficiency and convenience. Preaching, by default, morphed into a spiritual lecture or religious motivational speech in order to reach as many as possible with as little effort as possible. It became less about the people and more about the preacher. In my lifetime the rise of the personality preacher tattooed the church. Many people steeplechase and church hop in order to dance with the latest, greatest talker in town.

The problem is events aren't what people really need.

EVERYBODY'S GOT A HUNGRY HEART

Bruce Springsteen sang it best in his song "Hungry Heart": Every soul is starving. Deep down we're all naked and afraid, helpless and harassed. It just takes a crisis to reveal the reality and trouble to show the truth.

Most people are driven to church on their knees. Life has smacked them so far down they can only look up. The regulars already recognize this spiritual poverty, but the rest of the world requires some assistance. Nobody seeks pain or problems, but the best tonic for a thirsty soul is trial.

We're all very needy people.

Abraham Maslow theorized five basic hierarchal needs: physiological, safety, love/belonging, esteem, and self-actualization. Though at one time he viewed these needs as steps, he later conceded that self-actualization could happen despite whether the other needs were met or not. Psychologist William Glasser identified five basic human needs that resonate with Maslow: survival, love/belonging, power, fun, and freedom.

We all have hungry hearts. We struggle to survive, belong, choose, laugh, and feel positive about who we are and what we've become. These basic needs are authentic forces that drive human behavior, attitudes, and mindsets. If postmodern communicators are going to be effective, they will have to feed the needs.

SOUL FOOD

Okay, I'll confess: I love food.

Just the sight of a thick steak sounds alarms within my stomach. The smell of lasagna causes my gut to rumble. Even the sizzle of fajitas produces a tummy growl.

The full sensory experience motivates me to feed, but it's particularly powerful if I'm already hungry. Few stomachs growl when satiated.

Few souls do either.

Which is why we have to either feed the real need or create environments that draw those authentic desires to the surface. The problem is there's another easier and tempting way to motivate. We can also apply external pressure to force people to respond through guilt or gimmicks. I heard of a youth ministry in eastern Kentucky recently that doled out dollars to any teen who prayed, led worship, testified, or won a game. The little country church was a popular place…until the money ran out. Another church incentivizes their Sunday attendance with prize giveaways. Jesus passed out free fish sandwiches to everyone, while some churches today fish for disciples using prize patrols. Still others—too many others—employ guilt to motivate spiritual behaviors. And while guilt might push someone to follow Christ initially, it fails to persuade anyone for the long haul.

What people want is **Grace.**

What people need is **Community.**

What people desire is **Empowerment.**

What people appreciate is **Affirmation.**

What people love is **Pleasure.**

What people require is **Security.**

If you aim to authentically interact with postmoderns, you'll have to honor, embrace, and reveal their intrinsic human needs. Preaching, at its core, must be incarnational. Like Jesus, we need to leave our ivory pulpits and learn to walk with people. We must humbly lower ourselves to their world in order to build a bridge back to God. How do we touch today's postmodern? It's easier than you think, but you have to feed the need. You must satiate the GROWLS that rumble within their souls. You need to engineer environments that draw, engage, lead, and teach.

Essentially, there are six sacred spaces in which communicators interact. When someone is hungry, the stomach will rumble. Similarly, a starving soul G.R.O.W.L.S. beneath the craving of six human needs: Grace. Relationship. Ownership. Worth. Laughter. Security.

AMAZING GRACE, HOW SWEET THE SOUND

We love to sing "Amazing Grace." But, oh how we long to experience it. Grace is hard to define. It's messy. Unreasonable. Outlandish.

Ironically, I was deep in thought about how to present this idea to you when a central Oregon state trooper pulled me over for speeding. He clocked me at 66 miles per hour despite my cruise control locked at 65. I then learned I was in a construction zone and the speed limit was 50 miles per hour. He asked if I had seen the sign. To be honest, I had not. It wasn't until I turned the corner and saw construction barrels that I slowed down (at the same time he lit me up).

While the trooper was back in his vehicle to run my plates and registration, I tried hard to remember the last time I was pulled over for speeding (it was 1990!). I also knew I was wrong. Whether I saw the sign or not, I broke the limit. Whether my cruise control was working or not, even one mile over the limit, I violated the law. The officer returned with a long slip of paper. My heart sunk. This would not be good news.

"Mr. Chromey, I want to thank you for using your cruise control and staying close to the speed limit," the trooper said. "However, this is a well-marked construction zone and you have no excuse for missing the signs."

"Yes, officer," I replied, now fearing the worst.

"Because this is a construction zone, the fines are doubled and your violation will run you around $500," he continued.

I could feel the sweat roll off my forehead. I can't afford this right now.

"But today is your day," he announced. "I'm going to let you off with a warning. You need to slow down and pay attention."

I thanked the trooper profusely and pulled away grateful for the gift. Another speeding sinner freed from the penalty. But as amazing as that mercy was, it still wasn't grace. Mercy just lets me off. Grace presents a "free speeding for life" card. I shouldn't speed, but if I do and get caught, the card frees me. Sound crazy? Unreasonable? Amazing? That's grace.

And it's a primary spiritual need within every human being.

Whether you choose to believe or not, we all hunger for grace. We want to experience unconditional love and unbelievable blessing. We long to be granted mercy but dance wildly when we experience grace. The world is riddled with revenge, quid pro quo, and incentive-based motivation. Nothing is free. Everything has a string attached.

Jesus was a master communicator because he gracefully satisfied this deep human need. It was grace that drove him to touch contagious lepers, dine with tax collectors, and talk to promiscuous women. Jesus taught and preached with grace. His disciples were knuckleheads. I would've loved to hear Jesus' prayers, especially when he named names. It was grace that nailed him to a tree and said, "Father, forgive them, for they do not know what they are doing" (Luke 23:34).

> "Jesus straightened up and asked her, 'Woman, where are they? Has no one condemned you?'
>
> 'No one, sir,' she said.
>
> 'Then neither do I condemn you,' Jesus declared. 'Go now and leave your life of sin.'"
>
> —John 8:10-11

I'll be honest, it's hard to create a climate rich in grace.

Humans are naturally judgmental, divisive, critical, and hypocritical. Pharisees aren't fair, you see. And the church is filled with legalists and lawyers. We crave our rules and regulations, policies and procedures. The law is a friend to insure order and keep peace. Grace just muddies everything. Grace isn't fair. Grace is inclusive. Grace is loving.

To preach with grace is one thing. To engineer an environment where people sense forgiveness and freedom is another. The best strategy I've found is sensory. Create experiences where people *feel* forgiveness and freedom. Have people sit on their hands or bind them with string. Preach in the dark or blindfold your listeners. Distribute Band-Aids and ask people to share stories of healed scars. The best experiences use as many senses as possible. Grace has to be *felt* not dealt.

The Quest for Intimacy

I call it the "Rule of Threes." It takes but three minutes for a church visitor to decide whether they'll return. It requires three visits for someone to choose a church. It takes three months of regular attendance for a person to officially declare or pursue membership. And it's usually around year three when many agree it's time to move to a new church. At each point, the stickiness of a faith community determines attendance, affection, and, eventually, allegiance.

IF YOU DON'T BELONG, IT'S SO LONG

The second deep human need is for authentic relationships. Both Glasser and Maslow cite the importance of love and belonging. We all desire to connect and commune. We hunger to fit in and growl when we don't. Culturally, we see this need expressed in gangs, networks, fraternities, clubs, alliances, and tribes. Social networking has reinvented relationships into friends, followers, and fans. Online dating is a popular pastime. Reality television operates on the social connection.

Jesus was the original community organizer. Everywhere he went friendships formed. Jesus didn't rely on gimmicks or guilt to motivate community. He didn't promise prizes or wheel a deal. Instead, he built relationships through authenticity, attention, and affirmation. Jesus broke social norms to connect with the outcast. When he interacted with a Samaritan woman he violated multiple relational rules. She was a half-breed. She was female. She was living with a man who wasn't her husband. No young male single rabbi would've touched her with a ten-foot staff.

But Jesus wasn't confined by socially acceptable paradigms. And neither should you or your faith community.

> "My command is this: Love each other as I have loved you. Greater love has no one than this: to lay down one's life for one's friends. You are my friends if you do what I command. I no longer call you servants, because a servant does not know his master's business. Instead, I have called you friends, for everything that I learned from my Father I have made known to you."
>
> —John 15:12-15

Interactivity is a tool largely unexplored by today's preachers, but launching conversations is an explosive strategy to connect people and create friendships. A few years ago I preached for a church of 400 near Harrisburg, Pennsylvania. With the blessing of the leadership, I reinvented the preaching portion of the worship services. Instead of preaching from the stage, I moved to the floor and walked among the people. Every message contained an interactive element. My goal was to create three conversations in every sermon. I would speak for several minutes and then pause to allow the congregation to process the teaching.

To my surprise, nobody complained. In fact, people raved about the conversations. They enjoyed the intentional times of community. It was inspiring to witness children chatting it up with seasoned citizens, fathers speaking to sons, and newcomers meeting long-time members.

Surprisingly, my actual talk time was less than 20 minutes. The other 20 minutes was interaction and community. Application was particularly easy. Many preachers will make the applications, but I didn't. Instead I'd create a conversation that encouraged people to personalize the teaching. One particular message I remember well. After some teaching on evangelism, I released the congregation to spend several minutes connecting with someone they didn't know (or know well) and simply share their faith story.

My rule: If you leave the church experience without knowing yourself or someone else better, then we've failed.

HOUR OF POWER

I've got a secret for you: we're *all* control freaks.

We all want to be large and in charge. Every single person hungers to show power, to master control, and to enjoy choices. In a postmodern culture, the middles have collapsed. What used to be the bell curve is now the well curve, as power moved from the middle to the edges. Like the starfish, power has decentralized and intelligence spread throughout the entire organism. The emergence of Web culture has empowered every human with a smartphone, tablet, computer, mouse, or modem.

Consequently, the hunger for control and choice is exaggerated and amplified far beyond any previous time in history. People have always desired power, but it took the Internet to give everyone a voice. The average Joe can pen a post that changes the world. The average Jane can upload a video that goes virally global. This book will get lost unless people, like you, read and spread the word online (thank you!). As communicators we can no longer dismiss the people. We must share control and allow choice.

Jesus empowered people naturally. He never manipulated control, even when Satan tempted him to show his power in order to gain a kingdom (Matthew 4:1-11). Jesus freely gave his disciples choices. Peter didn't have to get out of the boat, and those who remained safely inside weren't condemned. He allowed a rich young ruler to walk away, a sinful woman to drown his feet with expensive perfume, and religious leaders to order his execution. Jesus relinquished control in order to reveal his power. He refused his own preferences in order to allow others to choose freely.

"When Jesus had called the Twelve together, he gave them power and authority to drive out all demons and to cure diseases, and he sent them out to proclaim the kingdom of God and to heal the sick...So they set out and went from village to village, proclaiming the good news and healing people everywhere."

—Luke 9:1-2, 6

Effective communication in a postmodern culture demands releasing the spotlight from you in order to flood your people to shine their own lights. Are there any testimonies in the house? Let them share. Several years ago I visited Andy Stanley's church in Atlanta. I came to hear him preach but was surprised with an Oprah-styled interview instead. Andy spoke with a man who lost everything, including his wife, to his pornography addiction. In this half-hour conversation, there were cheers, tears, and even fears expressed. And it's all because Andy Stanley shared the spotlight. Growing up, one of my favorite church services was "Sermon in a Sack" which allowed various church folk to preach an impromptu 5 minute devotional based on an object pulled from a sack.

The bottom line is people have sermons inside them, too. Let them out.

ONE OF A KIND!

The greatest evidence for a Divine creation is its awesome variety. No snowflake is alike. Are zebras white with black stripes or vice versa? And what was God thinking when he mashed a duck and beaver into a platypus?

Human beings are distinctly unique. The mold is broken after every birth. It's an unfathomable idea that no human is the same. We may carry some resemblances, like gender, height, age, ethnicity, or eye/skin/hair color, but we are all exceptionally, amazingly, beautifully different. This is why community and relationships are so messy. It's easy to connect the common, but when the differences are eternal, it's far more difficult.

Jesus affirmed personhood. Jesus called his disciples by name. He *personally* called Zacchaeus, a total stranger, from the tree (John 19:1-10). Peter was nicknamed "Pebbles" or "little stone" (Petros).[3] Jesus put dignity and value upon children, slaves, and women. The fact that he blessed children was outlandish. In the first century, few children survived to come of "age" (12 years old). The youngest person healed by Jesus was a 12-year-old. Rabbis would bless a boy at their circumcision and perhaps later in early adolescence, but it was truly radical to bless children.

Our human value is distinctly awarded at birth with our given names. Names mean something. We share first names with many and last names with family, but it's our middle name that separates us from all others. Think about it. The name that's often dismissed, even despised,

> "The one who enters by the gate is the shepherd of the sheep. The gatekeeper opens the gate for him, and the sheep listen to his voice. He calls his own sheep by name and leads them out. When he has brought out all his own, he goes on ahead of them, and his sheep follow him because they know his voice."
>
> —John 10:2-4

is the moniker that distinguishes. Our names can be sentimental, honorable, quirky, or ethnic-centric. I know a man named Ivan Odor and a woman known as Robin Wing. Now that's special!

As humans we possess unimaginable value. Our worth is priceless. We are so valuable that God incarnated into our mortal shell in order to build a bridge from earth to heaven. All religions have good doctrines, but only Christianity boasts a God who dwelt among man. It's what makes the Christian faith extraordinary. What does a soul cost? It's priceless enough for the one and only God to die in order to reclaim it.

Every person who hears your words must sense you value their presence. Of course, the smaller the crowd the easier this is to accomplish, but even in a thousand-seat auditorium it can be done. Eye contact is key. When we look people in the eye, we personally connect. I also like to use names if the group is smaller (less than 100 people). People are glued to your message simply when they hear their name. Of course, this isn't a license to throw a spotlight and tell a story without permission, but if you see John nodding his head in agreement, there's nothing wrong with saying, "Ain't that right, John? Yes, *you* know it is!"

The power of interaction also evokes feelings of personal worth. When individuals are allowed to share their stories, you're validating their personhood. We all want to feel special and relish whenever someone finds our story fascinating.

People matter to God. And without people you wouldn't have a message to give.

SMILES FOR MILES

Everyone loves to laugh.

Entertainment and enjoyment are two sides of the same hilarious coin. William Glasser sparked my thinking here when he listed "fun" as a basic human need. Fun is fundamental to human motivation. If we're not enjoying something, we lose interest. Pleasure is what pushes people to run marathons (or so I'm told). People garden, camp, bike, swim, race, ski, study, view, and serve because it's pleasing. When you enjoy something you are "in joy."

I think it would've been a blast to follow Jesus. How cool would it be to feed thousands of people with a boy's meager lunch? Or to walk on water? Or to catch a boatload of fish? I bet the disciples smiled when Jesus put a Pharisee in his place or gave a Sadducee the what-for. Jesus was a fun teacher. He didn't just read Scripture and offer intellectual commentary. Jesus told stories. The Kingdom of God is like a wedding party. Jesus came to give humans a laugh track. Heaven will be a hoot.

Pleasure is particularly important for communicators. When people laugh, the brain lights up like a Christmas tree. The synapses spark and people think deeper and more creatively. In fact, the number one characteristic of

> "At that time Jesus, full of joy through the Holy Spirit, said, 'I praise you, Father, Lord of heaven and earth.'"
>
> —Luke 10:21

memorable speakers is humor. Maybe that's why comedians can make a living telling jokes. It's definitely how people survive naked and afraid. He who laughs lasts.

Of course, you don't have to be Jay Leno or Jerry Seinfeld to be hilarious. But you must master the art of telling a joke, delivering a story, or adding a punch line. If nothing else, let others be funny for you. Show a humorous video clip. Ask someone to share a witty metaphor or comedic story. And always smile! Chuckle as you tell a story. Laughter is contagious. Just a little giggle can grow a mountain of mirth.

SAFE AND SECURE

The most basic of all needs is security or survival. We all need air, food, drink, light, heat, and other creature comforts. We also need to feel safe emotionally. When feelings are hurt, ignored, or abused, insecurity rises. In fact, we recall very little about what we heard in a sermon but can readily share how we felt.

This is why Jesus' ministry also included healing and helping miracles. He didn't have to feed a crowd of thousands, but they were hungry. He didn't have to heal the blind or lame but did. Everywhere Jesus preached he also assisted a person, a family, or a whole community to become better. The only time Scripture records Jesus crying was at the tomb of his friend Lazarus (John 11:35). Death was a mortal enemy. Jesus could heal disability, but he could not stop death. Even resurrecting Lazarus wouldn't stop it, for Lazarus would eventually die again. This broke Jesus' heart.

One of my favorite words for the worship area is "sanctuary." A sanctuary is a room of refuge, a home for the harassed, a place for the pursued. The only other space in my life that's even close is my house. My domicile is a safe place to dwell. I can escape home, lock the doors, shut the drapes, and hide. We all need a place to find sanctuary, don't we? So why do our worship "centers" and "auditoriums" (particularly in churches built since the 1970s) look more like lecture halls than living rooms? Is it not to "center" attention upon a few so the people can "hear" (auditory) a message?

I'm going to push a theological button right now. You may not like it, but I hope you'll hear me out. Are you ready? *God doesn't live in a house.* We don't go to God's house on Sunday. There's nothing sacred in any piece of furniture. There's nothing magical in the baptistery water. Yes, it's a sanctuary and it's sacred space when God's people gather, but it's not a temple. Paul made this point very clear to the Athenians: "The God who made the world and everything in it is the Lord of heaven and earth and does not live in temples built by human hands" (Acts 17:24).

He doesn't even show up on weekends.

God's divine space is the human heart. Wherever we are, God is.

A postmodern culture loves to create spiritual spaces. In fact, old-fashioned, stained-glass church buildings are popular purchases to reinvent as homes, coffee shops, and even bars. Pews and communion tables are trendy furniture buys. What makes postmoderns cringe is when the sacred is secularized. A worship concert is cheered, but truly intimate "living-room" styled, unplugged worship is far more attractive. And, yes, coffee and eats are welcomed.

This is why our messages must always have an upward lift. It's easy to create safe sacred space, but our sermon experiences must also fashion security. What do you want your congregation to feel? If I'm preaching on the miracle of the Incarnation, it's far better to speak among the people than from a separated stage. What does joy smell like? What does hope sound like? What does love taste like? What does faith look like? What does eternity feel like? If we can create secure, sensory experiences as part of our communication, the postmodern will respond.

In a nutshell, ditch the gimmicks (and guilt) and choose to feed the need: Grace. Relationship. Ownership. Worth. Laughter. Security.

Now I must eat. All this talk of food has made me hungry.

Endnotes

1. Bruce Springsteen, "Hungry Heart," *The River* (album), 1980.

2. While there are many examples of cathedral acoustics, the best one is the Mormon Tabernacle in Salt Lake City, Utah. This tortoise-shelled building is an architectural wonder, with acoustics so perfectly designed that a pin dropped at the pulpit can be heard in the back row!

3. Jesus personally changed Simon's name to Peter (Mark 3:16). In the Greek, Peter (Petros) mean "little rock" or stone. Jesus will create a pun when he talks about how the church is built on a rock (Matthew 16:18): "And I tell you that you are Peter (Petros: stone), and on this rock (Petra: massive foundation stone) I will build my church."

Chapter Eight:
GO DEEP AND GO HOME

"I have a lot more to say about this, but it is hard to get it across to you since you've picked up this bad habit of not listening. By this time you ought to be teachers yourselves, yet here I find you need someone to sit down with you and go over the basics on God again, starting from square one—baby's milk, when you should have been on solid food long ago! Milk is for beginners, inexperienced in God's ways; solid food is for the mature, who have some practice in telling right from wrong."

—Hebrews 5:11-14, *The Message*

A mystery of titanic proportions captivated the world's attention in early 2014. On March 8, a Malaysian Airlines flight with 239 souls on board simply vanished without a trace. In the weeks to follow, the largest global plane hunt in history scoured the vast Indian Ocean for any sign of life, debris. or fuel slick. For some reason the plane went dark just after takeoff and neither radar nor satellite technology offered any explanation. The mystery was magnified by speculations of terrorism, possibly by the captain or passengers, but no theory truly satisfied.

How does a plane just disappear from radar? How does it crash into the ocean without leaving a single shred of debris or the telltale fuel slick?

The only resolution to the enigma lay within the plane's data recorder, or black box. The search for a "ping" from this device was frantic given the recorder's limited battery life. A smattering of pings and some large debris (never confirmed as Malaysian Flight 370) renewed hope but in the end were fruitless. The hunt shifted in mid-April to a deep-sea scour of the ocean floor that many likened to finding a purple toothpick somewhere in the Colorado Rockies.

Sometimes life's greatest mysteries are buried on the bottom.

And the questions must run equally deep to uncover them.

THE INFORMATION OCEAN

The postmodern problem is a life flooded with information. Sound bites, breaking news, tweets, instant messages, emails, Facebook shares, spam, texts, and dozens of other communication lines inundate our inboxes, screens, and newsfeeds. At our fingertips lies a Google search that can unearth millions of possible solutions. Our television channel lineup boasts hundreds of channels with thousands of shows. Thanks to smartphones we're intricately linked to everything happening all the time. Nothing escapes the connected. News finds us. Deals hunt us. People follow us. It's a bit creepy when you think about it.

This sea of information becomes a tsunami of triviality that tries our souls with deep questions: *Where did I come from? Why am I here? Where am I going?*

And like a black box sunk deep beneath the ocean, the answers to these queries lie in wait for our discovery. On the surface of superficiality, our culture desperately scours, searches, and sinks various lines hoping to hear the ping of peace but is left wondering why serenity remains so elusive. We hunt for happiness, longing for joy, but only accumulate the debris of debt and washed wreckage of stuff. In our heart of hearts we know we were destined for flight but spend most of our lives drowning in fear, worry, and regret.

It's a desperate dilemma for the postmodern mind.

On one hand all of life's answers can be carried in your back pocket, while on the other it's so difficult to discern what's real or relevant. In the modern world, the purpose of education was knowledge. The more you knew the better you felt, right? But in a postmodern culture, knowledge is practically a nemesis. We have no problem knowing stuff. Our problem is the veracity of the information. *Is it true? Can it be proven? Is it useful?*

Have you ever considered how much information flies all around us? Here are a few factoids (one of which *may* be false):

- Ninety percent of the world's data was created in just 2 years.[1]
- Every 2 days we generate as much information as was previously accumulated from the dawn of history until 2003.[2]
- Every minute 48 hours of video is uploaded to YouTube, 347 blogs are posted by WordPress, and more than 100,000 tweets are sent.[3]
- Every minute 2 million searches are made using Google, 684,478 Facebook users share content, and 204,166,667 messages are emailed.[4]

Did you guess the potentially false one? Well, be patient, and I'll reveal the answer later.

I'VE GOT NEWS FOR YOU

I saw a Prius the other day sporting a "Fox News is bad news for America" bumper sticker. Right next to it was a Honda with an "I don't believe the liberal media" decal. I had to laugh. It's no wonder postmoderns get their news from Comedy Central. When it comes to news (and sermons), there's no such thing as a "no spin" zone.

The recognition of this reality is crucial when preaching to postmodern generations. They are walking cyber encyclopedias and can access information faster than you can say "repent." As we talked about in the last chapter, postmoderns are skeptical. They embrace doubt and incredulity and struggle with anyone who can take the majesty and magnificence of God and reduce him to a theological thimble of truth (which may or may not be correct).

This is disconcerting for the pastor who just spent hours in study and believes his message is "fair and balanced" (objective). How could anyone doubt his hermeneutic or criticize his conclusions? But I bet you never imagined your listeners instantly accessing information that counters your well-studied statements. I routinely Google information during sermon time. I like to verify a fact or confirm something said.

The other problem is error. If you miscommunicate or misstate in the smallest degree, your whole message is now suspect. Some people have a low tolerance for error, particularly from preachers who claim to speak for God. After all, if you can't get it right on one point, how can I trust the rest of your revelation to me, whether by analysis or application?

In an information age, the most important cognitive skill is critical thinking. The Gutenberg revolution engineered a literate culture. However, a cyber world demands discernment. Facts—just like images—are easily doctored, altered, and manipulated. In fact, the first casualty of breaking news is always the truth.[6] Just because we think we know doesn't mean we know everything. And just because we think we know everything doesn't mean we really know *everything*.

Modern communication focused on facts and preached propositions. The facts were indisputable; therefore, the conclusions were undeniable. If the science proved the thesis, then it was true. If the network news said it happened a certain way, then it's trusted information. If someone with letters behind their name said it was right, then there's no question. If the denomination or founding father or bishop claimed it was good, then there's nothing to debate. Modern boxes squeezed out the search for answers through control and censorship. What wasn't stated is as important as what was.

WHY JOHNNY DOESN'T KNOW THE BIBLE

Several years ago Jay Leno did a humorous "man on the street" segment about what people knew about the Bible. The responses ranged from the silly to the stupid, but most revealed a tragic illiteracy of biblical stories. In general, the American public is woefully ignorant of the Scriptures. Sadly, most churchgoers aren't far behind.

Of course, it's easy to point a finger.

But I do think preaching is part of the problem.

Sitting Through God School

In the beginning, when the Church-As-We-Know-It was invented, somebody asked, "How should we design this thing?"

I imagine someone looked around and said, "Our job is to propagate the faith. We should do that like you propagate other subjects—like literature or mathematics or history."

Most likely, the committee chair said, "Good idea." So they set up the Church-As-We-Know-It like you would any other academic institution. With faith as the subject, they found learned professor-types to stand before the unlearned and dispense information. The lecture halls were set up with pupil seating in neat rows facing the learned ones. It was the professors' job to lecture. It was the pupils' job to sit still, be quiet, and appear to be listening.

And so it was that the Church-As-We-Know-It became an academic institution.

The early designers were successful in establishing faith as one more academic subject. Even to this day the people recognize faith—or religion, as they call it—one more subject to study. And the Church-As-We-Know-It does everything it can to foster this academic reputation:

- The people gather at the appointed time, file in, sit in rows, and stare silently at the lecturer.
- The preacher thumps a book and refers to the "text" of the day.
- The "teaching pastor" provides a printed outline with fill-in-the-blanks for easy answers.
- The grown-ups go to Bible "study."
- The young ones go to age-graded Sunday "school."
- Sunday school "curriculum" utilizes word scrambles and other schoolish busywork.
- They call the teenagers "students."

- The Christian "education" department organizes "classes."
- Kids compete in Bible "quizzing."
- Discipleship means attending a 6-week "course."
- "Deep" teaching involves lectures filled with layers of biblical facts and historical minutiae.
- They call the church property a "campus."
- The sign out front says, "A Strong Bible-Teaching Church."

Academic institutions serve their purpose. Subjects get taught. But when it comes to the church, there's one problem. Faith is not a subject.

Faith is a relationship.[7]

—Thom Schultz, *Holy Soup*

Since World War II, the sermon has evolved from being a theological treatise into various expressions of self-improvement pop psychology, culturally clever themes, and feel-good inspirational topics.[8] It's possible on any given Sunday in America to hear a message that simply sprinkles Scriptures over spiritual ideas like candy. Such superficiality is winsome and popular, but like flotsam and jetsam, it rarely moves listeners to profound insight or productive life change. We have raised a generation of biblical illiterates—many who emerged out of our children's and youth ministries of the 1980s and 1990s—who view God's Word as confusing, strange, and mysterious. As the Hebrew writer penned, they should be chewing on ribeye but don't have the teeth to bite into anything but a milkshake.

It's nothing new.

The greatest enemy of spiritual maturity has always been ignorance. What we don't know stunts and stalls our faith development.

Postmodern communicators will need to dive deep.

If the church has any chance to resurrect biblical literacy among believers, then the sermon must unleash critical thinking. I can hear the "amens" now! We need more meat and less milk. It's time to preach the Word. Yes, but don't miss my point. Preaching the meat won't matter if people can't swallow it or, worse, choke on it and leave with a bad taste about Christianity.

I went to church last night and heard a powerful message on the "facts of the Resurrection." The explanations were clear. The illustrations helpful. The use of Greek and rhetoric was flawless. But the 30-something guy sitting next to me was sound asleep (and I wasn't too far behind). This pastor is a 99 percenter: 99 percent content, 1 percent application. He's a professor in the pulpit, and clearly people enjoy his exegesis and verse-by-verse expository messages.

But few remember a word after 24 hours. The Word was planted, but the wind of time blows it away because it has no root in the life of the hearer. Those who preach to the head will always miss the heart.

On the other hand there's another pastor I know.

He's a 90 percenter: 90 percent application and 10 percent content. His messages are interesting and inspiring, enjoyable and empowering. He recently preached a sermon series on marriage that most found very helpful. This pastor doesn't impress you with Greek but with grace. You don't always walk away feeling like you learned something, but you'll always leave with a smile. You feel good. He's like Oprah in the pulpit, and people clearly love his op-eds on life, culture, and faith.

But few still feel a thing after 24 hours.

In reality, neither of these pastors—even though they preach to thousands every Sunday—are attracting postmoderns. Both preachers stand before a sea of white, bald, and wrinkled.

You see, the postmodern doesn't go to church, *if* they go, for a lecture or a motivational message. They go to *experience* God. They want to hear him speak and then reflect deeply on the Word. A sermon packed with insight but soft on application is boring, but a homily rich in inspiration that lacks depth proves rather superficial. Postmoderns want to be amused *and* moved to think deeply. But the kicker? They are wired by Web and mobile technology to think deeply through conversation not oratorical rhetoric.

There's nothing wrong with sharing Greek meanings and outlining historical and cultural contexts. People of all ages love to learn something new. You should want your audiences to think. However, in an entertainment culture, we must also embrace fun as a tool, or, as I call it: edu-tainment. I'll reinforce a point with a clip from a popular movie or television show. I'll explain a difficult idea with a cultural metaphor. For those who criticize amusement, they seem to forget this is how Jesus told parables. They were enjoyable. People love a great story, and Jesus was a master storyteller. He revealed heavenly mysteries through earthly activities.

I'm convinced that in order to reach postmodern generations we must be insightful *and* inspirational, deep *and* wide, educational *and* entertaining. We need to be 50/50: 50 percent content and 50 percent application. If you require a cultural example, watch *The Dr. Oz Show*. This daytime television doctor has been a boon for health and medicine, especially for women. You always learn something new from Dr. Mehmet Oz, but you also enjoy *how* he teaches you through objects, demonstrations, videos, and testimonies. More importantly, he creates conversation.

How can preaching be more like Dr. Oz? How can we go deep? We do it by going home. Go deep *and* go home.

It's time to play ball.

TAKE ME OUT TO THE BALL GAME

If God ever had a hand in designing a sport, it would be baseball. No other game compares. Some sports may be more strategic (like football). Some sports may require more stamina (like basketball). Some sports might demand special skills (like golf or hockey). But no sport weaves all these into a single game like baseball.

Baseball is a thinking man's sport.

That's because you actually have time to think. In football and basketball, the tyranny of the clock forces quick decisions, but in baseball there's time to reflect, react, or revise. Critics

> "No game in the world is as tidy and dramatically neat as baseball, with cause and effect, crime and punishment, motive and result, so cleanly defined."[9]
> —Paul Gallico

will call it a slow sport, but it's that slowness which creates conversation. Have you ever tried to talk at a football or basketball game? Baseball is a great first date. Baseball also creates special strategies. For example, because every batter is studied and mapped, the opposing team knows his tendencies and shifts the defense to remove holes. No other sport honors its history like the grand old game. The past is alive, and every current player is weighed against the ghosts of previous eras. Baseball is past, present, and future.

> "This is a game to be savored, not gulped. There's time to discuss everything between pitches or between innings."[10]
> —Bill Veeck

Baseball is also entertaining.

No other sport provides the opportunity for more souvenirs. People bring gloves to the game and pray for foul balls. The senses come alive at a baseball game.

The majestic spread of the green grass inside colossal coliseums. The crack of the bat, the pop of the leather, and the bark of vendors. The taste of brats, cotton candy, and pretzels. The smell of fresh air, sweet treats, and beer. The high five with a friend after a home run or singing with the crowd during the seventh inning stretch. Baseball is fun. It's fun to watch but even more enjoyable to experience live.

While all major sports have experienced attendance declines, particularly professional football and basketball, baseball continues to hold its own even in a recessive economy. I don't believe that's a coincidence.

As a game, baseball is most like life. No ballpark is the same. Outside the diamond base paths, everything else is unique from the ivy outfield in Wrigley to the "green monster" in Fenway to Petco Park in San Diego. Unlike the struggle on the gridiron, which resembles a war, baseball is about coming full circle and touching home. It features three bases and a plate. You end where you start. In baseball you run a path like the seasons. First base resembles spring. Second like summer. Third like fall. And home like winter. Since the sport follows the seasons, it makes sense. Baseball opens in the spring and closes in the fall, resting at home in the winter.

This organic philosophy is what's sorely needed in the pulpit.

Life is seasonal and developmental. We remember more of what we experience. Our lives follow the path of the seasons. Our passions blossom in the springtime of our youth. Purpose is revealed during the heat of young adulthood. Wisdom falls in middle age, and our legacies are left like footprints in the white snow of old age.

Consequently, sermons that follow rigid, point-driven plans fall flat, especially to the younger generations. Many preachers stick to a speaking plan regardless of whether people need or want it. I learned this lesson a few years ago. I was preaching a series on the book of Acts and, after a month, learned my messages were not what the congregation needed. I listened to the people, despite my personal enthusiasm for Acts, and switched to Philippians. Those sermons were just what the Holy Spirit ordered.

RUNNING THE BASES

Go deep *and* go home.

That's the secret to reach the postmodern mind. Go deep and draw out the hidden insights from God's Word, then take them home through conversation that unleashes critical thinking.

In the mid-1950s, Benjamin Bloom theorized a process for learning that he called a taxonomy of cognitive objectives. He proposed that critical thinking follows a path: knowledge, comprehension, application, analysis, synthesis, and evaluation.[12] In my Christian education courses, I reduced these six levels to the Three R's: Recall, Reproduce, and Reinvent. Bloom's taxonomy is helpful to communicators and particularly to preachers who seek to reach postmodern audiences. The problem with the majority of preaching is self-evident: It's largely lower-order thinking (knowledge, comprehension, application). In order to massage higher-level critical thinking, the listener must move from passive to active.

Postmoderns don't just want to go deep. They also want to go *home*. They hunger for opportunities to dialogue and think critically about their faith, culture, and life. Every social media outlet is a treasure trove of conversations about faith and culture. My argument throughout this book has been a call to reinvent the sermon around a conversation. Now I'm going to show you how it's done.

We'll use the game of baseball to do it.

FIRST BASE: RECALL

The lowest and most primal level of cognitive activity is the accumulation of knowledge and understanding of facts. The difference between knowledge and comprehension is as great as the momentum between zero and one. Facts are flying around us all the time. They only stick when we comprehend them.

In every sermon there needs to be a simple outline of the text or topic. We need to define terms, explain issues, recite truths, identify problems, and interpret contexts. This is where your study of a passage is critical. You have to know your text and hold expertise in your topic. But if the listeners don't understand, then all you've done is talk into the air. You've heard of air guitar? I call this "air preaching"!

How do you know if the congregation understands?

Well, you ask them.

And this is where your first conversation emerges. The purpose of this initial dialogue is to produce comprehension. So after you introduce the text or topic (5 to 10 minutes), you ask "meaning" types of questions and invite your congregation to discuss what is happening within a particular text or topic.

Question Examples

Text: The Prodigal Son

Comprehension Questions: What does it mean for this son to be called a "prodigal"? Briefly retell this story, as you understand it. What do each of the characters represent to you?

Topic: God's Love (I Corinthians 13)

Comprehension Questions: Review each characteristic of love and explain what it means to you. How would you define love? What does the idea that "God loves you" mean to you?

Face the facts: Until your people understand the story, they haven't made it safely to first base. All they've done is cognitively struck out, popped, or grounded out (resulting in looks of boredom). Some may criticize this process and question whether it's worth sacrificing sermon time for a few minutes of interaction on meaning, but I would argue, along with learning specialists, that we remember more of what we talk about. Don't assume the takeaways will be less, because if you can master comprehension questions, your people will recall the story or topic better.

SECOND BASE: RESPOND

A lot of Sunday sermons leave men and women on base, particularly first.

In fact, most expository sermons are first-basers by their nature. They dissect the passage and, if communicated well, produce insight and understanding. But that's where it ends. The listener is left hanging.

Bloom argued that once we understand information it must be applied before we can embrace higher critical thinking. The problem is application happens best when done by the person in the chair, and there are two equally poor extremes. On one hand, many preachers make all the applications and deliver them like a pepperoni pizza. But, on the other hand, especially in some theological circles, many feel it's the Holy Spirit's role to deliver the pie. Just present the facts and get out of the way.

I have no doubt the Holy Spirit can spark personal applications. How many times have you wondered if the preacher was reading your private journal? That's the Holy Spirit at work, plowing truth through your life and nudging you to consider changes. Nevertheless, I still believe God works best through prepared moments and opportunities for people to put hands and feet to the pastor's message.

It's just unfortunate that most preachers steal the application time for their own purpose. It's not intentional and wholly innocent, but if we want our congregation to reach second base and think deeper about our text or topic, we need another conversation. This one might require a few more minutes (no more than 5 minutes), but during this interaction, people make your message applicable to their context. So again, after a few moments of transition (5 to 7 minutes tops), you open the floor back up for conversation. The questions are pointed and direct. In fact, sometimes it's better to encourage people to find a new partner, someone other than their spouse, child, or parent. Application demands transparency, and that's not always best with someone you know well.

Application Examples

Text: The Prodigal Son

Application Questions: When have you acted like a prodigal? Have you ever felt like the older brother? When? Why? Are there any prodigals in your life right now? How are you responding?

Topic: God's Love (1 Corinthians 13)

Application Questions: How well do you live up to these "love" standards? How have you experienced these characteristics? Who has loved you like this? Why is it so hard for you to love completely like Paul writes?

Application questions can also be *practiced* during the message time. I preached a message on sharing your faith and invited the congregation to interact with individuals they didn't know well and briefly share their faith story (in 3 to 5 minutes). It was a powerful moment! Another time I asked everyone to encourage one another and affirm unique spiritual gifts they observed in others. Any time you can personally apply (through interaction) the better.

By the way, the conversion to a conversational format will take time, so don't give up if you encounter resistance or even rejection. The younger the overall age, the easier the change will be, but many older adults will also welcome opportunities to dialogue about their faith and apply it to life. It's a just a new way to experience church, and change rarely feels good or is easy.

THIRD BASE: REPRODUCE

I can honestly say I can't think of any sermon (in recent memory) that moved people to third base thinking or analysis. If people think this critically about a message it only happens after they leave the building. The nature of analysis is helped by dialogue and demands time for reflection, especially if an insight is new, questionable, or ironic.

But what if we infused a brief conversation in every message that provoked deeper thought? And this dialogue forced listeners to grapple with the content through the lens of their experience. And it encouraged analysis of the text, synthesis of the message, and an overall evaluation of life, faith, and culture.

When our messages are reproduced in the heart of our hearers, faith comes alive. The difference between second base (application) and third base (reproduction) is as great as a Band-Aid and a tattoo! A Band-Aid is applied and has a momentary sticking to a person's life. It may even produce security and some healing. But a tattoo is a permanent reminder. It's under the skin not topical. You can't lose it, because you have willingly inked your life with its influence.

A popular movie a few years ago was *Memento*, starring Guy Pearce. It is the story of a man who, due to a brain injury, cannot retain short-term memory. He can remember everything that happened up to his accident but only several minutes after that moment. To compensate for his disability, he develops an ingenious strategy of Polaroids (with handwritten comments), Post-It notes, and, for the most important information, permanent tattoos. The problem for the character is two-fold: How does he chronicle his memories effectively, and how will he trust his narrative. The movie contains two stories happening at the same time (one in reverse and one in forward motion), which, ultimately, collide at the end of the film.

Our listeners have short-term memory. It's a spiritual disability. And if we don't provide ways for our listeners to critically think about our messages, they won't remember them. We need to give them cameras to shoot deep into their lives. We need to distribute Post-It note moments to interact with other believers about faith. And, for those willing, we must provide opportunity for them to tattoo their lives permanently. What happens in church today is that it's the preacher who stands up, displays, and explains his tattoos. It's time to flip that!

Analysis/Synthesis/Evaluation Examples

Text: The Prodigal Son

Analysis/Synthesis/Evaluation Questions: In the story, which character is most like the majority of people in your circle of friends? Why? Are there other stories in Scripture that resemble this story? Which ones? Which character in this story was hurt the most? Why? In your opinion, what is the central theme of this story and why was it so important for Jesus to tell it?

Topic: God's Love (I Corinthians 13)

Analysis/Synthesis/Evaluation Questions: Of the various descriptive statements about love in this chapter, which one is most important? Least important? Why? Can you think of other stories in Scripture that serve as applications for each characteristic? Paul says, "Faith, hope and love…the greatest of these is love" (1 Corinthians 13:13). Do you agree? Why or why not?

NOTE: Higher order questions are the most difficult to write and very few can write them well. However, most educators have been trained in this skill (while few preachers have). If you struggle to write questions like the ones above, I would encourage you to find an individual (or two or three) to serve on your sermon prep team and do nothing but write award-winning questions.

HOME PLATE: REINVENT

Anyone who knows baseball or has played the game understands the most productive scoring spot is third base. If you can get to third, there's a fairly good chance you'll score. But, as I've mentioned, most Sunday sermons are singles and doubles at best. They leave the soul (and mind) stuck at second. In baseball statistics it's called a LOB or "left on base." The church is in the business of manufacturing runs, and LOBs are missed scoring opportunities.

The difference between reproduction and reinvention is small, and it simply means folding in a "life change" challenge at the end of every message. This is a take "home" invitation to live out the passage within the hearer's context. Jesus explained clearly that if you *love* me (heart) you will *obey* (life) my commands. Preaching isn't only about tickling the mind with insight or even sparking the heart with inspiration. Ultimately, our messages must create life change.

On the Day of Pentecost, Peter preached a profound message packed with prophecy and biblical instruction that caused his listeners to be "cut to the heart." His sermon created such a thirst that the crowd blurted out, "What shall we do [to be saved]?"

Life Challenge Examples

Text: The Prodigal Son

Life Challenge: Reflect on this story and your current situation. Of the characters, which are you most like? Now, in the coming week, identify and practice positive behaviors that will reflect a prodigal son come home or a father's wait or give up an older brother's jealousy. Write what happens and share your takeaways on our church's Facebook page.

Topic: God's Love (1 Corinthians 13)

Life Challenge: Choose one of the following exercises or experiences to do in the coming week:

1. Memorize 1 Corinthians 13, and share with at least three friends.

2. Habitually practice love with everyone you meet: patience, kindness, forgiving of wrong, etc. Share your experiences on our Facebook page.

3. Create a YouTube video or write a blog or draw/paint a picture that makes 1 Corinthians 13 come to life. As much as possible, make it a personal testimony, and then share with your friends on Facebook.

NOTE: As much as possible, give choices. You will have a better response. Secondly, create journaling space for listeners to demonstrate life change and then testify to how they're growing spiritually. A Facebook page or interactive forum on your church's website is a great way to know if your messages are "hitting home."

(Acts 2:37). And Peter told them very simply: "Repent and be baptized" (2:38). They already believed the message—but now they wanted to *live* it, and 3,000 people were baptized that day (2:41). That's going home.

A life challenge is a simple tag on every message you can create to direct life change. It must be observable, dynamic, and productive. A powerful life challenge will identify specific behaviors to push the hearers to take it "home."

GO DEEP AND GO HOME

If we have any hope of interacting with emerging postmodern generations, we'll have to create a haven for critical thought and push hearers to live their faith in community and conversation daily. For if we cannot tattoo life-changing Christianity under the skin of people, the Band-Aids will eventually slip off and be forgotten. Perception, inspiration, and transformation are the trinity of change.

The church is a change agent. Our messages must produce change.

We can't afford to strike out anymore. It's time to swing for the fences.

P.S. What was the false statement among the factoids? It's the statistic that more information is generated every two days than from the dawn of history until 2003. Google CEO Eric Schmidt first promoted this popular Internet myth at the 2010 Techonomy conference, but it may not be true.[13]

Endnotes

1. SINTEF, "Big Data, for better or worse: 90% of world's data generated over last two years." ScienceDaily, 22 May 2013, www.sciencedaily.com/releases/2013/05/130522085217.htm.

2. MG Siegler, "Eric Schmidt: Every 2 Days We Create As Much Information As We Did Up To 2003," TechCrunch, 4 August, 2010, http://techcrunch.com/2010/08/04/schmidt-data/.

3. Neil Spencer, "How Much Data Is Created Every Minute?" Visual News, 19 June, 2012, http://www.visualnews.com/2012/06/19/how-much-data-created-every-minute/.

4. Ibid.

5. MG Siegler, "Eric Schmidt: Every 2 Days We Create As Much Information As We Did Up To 2003," TechCrunch, 4 August, 2010, http://techcrunch.com/2010/08/04/schmidt-data/.

6. For an interesting exercise in news and facts, Google "when the news gets it wrong" and check out the results.

7. Thom Schultz, "Sitting Through God School," *Holy Soup* (blog), April 30, 2014, http://holysoup.com/2014/04/30/sitting-through-god-school/.

8. A simple overview of modern Protestant preaching can be reduced to three chapters or eras: 1) Reformation (1500-1700); 2) Great Awakening (1700-1950); and 3) Evangelical (1950-present). During the Reformation, preaching focused upon doctrinal inculcation and themes related to grace, God's sovereignty, and reforming errors. In the Great Awakening, preaching shifted to the enlightenment of sinners, God's wrath, and restoring Christian faith and practice. After World War II, evangelicalism emerged behind radio and television preachers who were more topical, application-driven, and focused on "soul winning."

9. "Paul Gallico Quotes," Goodreads, http://www.goodreads.com/author/quotes/92064.Paul_Gallico.

10. "Bill Veeck Quote," izquotes.com, http://izquotes.com/quote/291898.

11. "Baseball Sports Quotes," Top End Sports, http://www.topendsports.com/sport/baseball/quotes.htm.

12. Patricia Armstrong, "Bloom's Taxonomy," *Center for Teaching, Vanderbilt University,* http://cft.vanderbilt.edu/guides-sub-pages/blooms-taxonomy/.

13. Robert Moore penned an interesting blog on why Eric Schmidt is wrong. Of course, the follow-up comments are as insightful as the blog itself. In the end? You decide: http://blog.rjmetrics.com/2011/02/07/eric-schmidts-5-exabytes-quote-is-a-load-of-crap/.

Chapter Nine:
BLOODLINES

> "When he was at the table with them, he took bread, gave thanks, broke it and began to give it to them. Then their eyes were opened and they recognized him, and he disappeared from their sight. They asked each other, 'Were not our hearts burning within us while he talked with us on the road and opened the Scriptures to us?'"
>
> —Luke 24:30-32

> "Jesus said to them, 'Very truly I tell you, unless you eat the flesh of the Son of Man and drink his blood, you have no life in you.'"
>
> —John 6:53

It was the morning of January 26, 2005.

And it was shaping up to be just another typical commute for 44-year-old John Phipps and the millions of other Los Angeles workers. He didn't normally go to work this early but had been called into a job at his aerospace plant in Burbank. When the father of three boarded his train he couldn't possibly have known a suicidal Juan Manual Alvarez had parked his sport utility vehicle on the train tracks several miles away in the Glendale, California suburb.

It was only minutes to mayhem.

Details about what happened are sketchy, but Alvarez evidently changed his mind and abandoned his car just prior to the collision with the oncoming train—a train that carried John Phipps and hundreds of other passengers. Alvarez's selfish act killed 11 people and injured more than 200, including John Phipps, who lay in his own blood with head and groin injuries. As he floated in and out of consciousness, saying, "Why me, Lord?" to himself, all Phipps could think about was his family.

Losing blood and life, Phipps desperately desired to leave his final thoughts. He had no paper or pen. All he had was his own blood to finger a simple message on the back of a train chair: *"I ♥ my kids. I ♥ Leslie."* His wife later said, "Hallmark is never going to top that," and she's right.[1] Soon after Phipps scrawled his haunting message, rescuers reached him and found that bloody note. His survival and recovery is nothing short of miraculous.

There's power in the blood.

And preaching that is powerful must be equally bloody. It will be messy. It'll scrawl simple messages of love and hope and faith onto ordinary things to inspire extraordinary insights and applications. When we preach, we give blood. We donate a pint of power. We transfuse the mystery of Life from our heart to our hearers.

Dr. Leonard Sweet, in his book on preaching to the postmodern mind, penned a similar refrain:

> I can think of no better definition of preaching than "giving blood." Of the three traditional ways of making a living—mud, blood, and grease—preaching involves all three: the mud pies of creativity, the blood bank of living in the Word, and the grease pit of hard work and dirty hands. But of the three, giving blood is the defining metaphor.[2]

Preaching is blood-letting. It's being splashed by the blood, washed in the blood, and changed by the blood. Just the thought of being baptized in blood sounds gruesome, edgy, and scary. In today's antiseptic, sterile culture, blood is a precious yet isolated commodity. It's drained with procedure, boxed by type, and administered under doctor's order. With the emergence of AIDS, we're very aware that someone else's blood can kill you.

Maybe that's why most preaching today is blood-less.

When was the last time you heard a sermon that scared you to death? When was the last time a church service was so bloody you left feeling the pain of wounds wide open? When was the last time you experienced the splash of blood—from the Living Word of God—upon your life? When was the last time you left church feeling woozy and drained from the emotional bloodletting?

I doubt it's happened lately.

From the smallest to the largest Protestant churches in America, the blood of Christ is a rare type that's kept safe from any spill. We don't want any bloody messes, especially in church. That would be far too dangerous, gross, and undignified. I remember how a church member once chided our worship leader for choosing the standard hymn, "Are You Washed in the Blood?" He found the idea repulsive. "Can't we sing something a bit more *nice?*" he asked.

For the past 500 years, preaching (like church and churchianity) has slowly become "nice" and sterile, packed in glass points and administered only by the qualified. Sunday morning sermons are safe places to receive a transfusion. And since most preachers only service one type, the steeplechase to find the best blood for an individual's taste is a constant game.

Meanwhile, in the real world, everything is dipped in blood. A rare or medium steak drips in blood and is a favorite choice. In fact, bloody foods like "blodplättar" (bloody pancakes), "Pig's Blood Ice Cream Sundae," and blood sausage are in vogue. Vampire shows (*True Blood*) and movies (*The Twilight Series*) are popular. In the news media, if it bleeds it leads. The sports that attract often are bloody, whether it's ringside, center court, or 50-yard line. In my iTunes library, I currently have 163 songs with "blood" in the title, including "Bad Blood," "Sunday Bloody Sunday," "Hot Blooded," "The Blood Song," and "Nothing But the Blood."

Blood runs rampant in our culture.

The most popular television crime shows include blood investigations. Slasher movies remain a staple, as do video games that splatter blood (particularly your own). The most popular Jesus movie was *The Passion of the Christ*, and it was R-rated for violence and blood. A current trend among the elite is for mothers to eat their own placenta. A medical procedure known as biotherapy involves the use of leaches to suck blood and devour diseased flesh.

I hope I've made my pint…I mean, point.

And yet the place where the blood should run deep and wide—the church—is largely anemic and absent. We've leeched our worship experience and preaching and produced a "nice" sanitary place. In my tribe, which weekly celebrates the Lord's Supper, it's a rare thing to hear the word "blood" attached to the drive-by ritual. We don't want to drink of the blood. And nobody wants to hear, sing, speak, or learn about blood either. It's not unusual for communion to take less time than the announcements.

I think it's time to open a vein and bleed for real.

We've been squeamish about blood for too long. Christianity, by its very nature, is bloody. The blood of a crucified Messiah.[3] The blood of Old Covenant sacrifices.[4] The blood of a New Covenant.[5] The blood of martyrs.[6] The blood of the Eucharist drink.[7] The blood of forgiveness.[8] The bloody betrayal of Judas.[9] The blood of a coming Messiah.[10] When worship bleeds, people experience the Throne. When preaching bleeds, people encounter Christ.

In my last chapter, I shared the process for interactive preaching. Now, I'd like to reveal the bloody work of experiential communication. Just understand that it'll be messy, painful, and you will get wet on this ride.

A SEMIOTIC REVOLUTION

If you've paid careful attention throughout this book, you've noticed I've relied on stories and images to explain my ideas. The postmodern mind thrives on metaphors and visuals, but if they're done wrong, displayed poorly, or interpreted badly, it's a turn off. In 20 years of instructing college students how to teach and preach, I've learned they're not persuaded by a PowerPoint and view many movie clips as unimpressive. In fact, they find most professors' and preachers' visuals to be distasteful altogether.

What we need is a semiotic revolution.

The ability to read the image and translate it with power and purpose is what inspires. It's a new skill, known as semiotics, that few preaching schools and classes even teach, but it's time we did. Len Sweet explains:

> Sermons that point to Christ through stories and images make use of 'semiotics.' Semiotics is best defined as the ability to read and convey 'signs,' where a 'sign' (be it an image, gesture, sound, object, or word) is something that stands for something else. Semiotics is about pointers, not points. You can't point to Jesus if you're trying to make Jesus fit your point...

> A semiotic sermon reads the signs of what God is up to in the world, connects those signs in people's lives with the Jesus story, and then communicates the gospel by connecting people in relationship to Jesus through stories, images, and gestures.[11]

Semiotic and symbiotic are twins to powerful communication. Our ability to connect signs, build bridges, and open doors will lead to connectivity and community. Too many preachers are blind and deaf. They can't see the signs, and they can't hear their people, especially the younger generations. Consequently, they produce bloodless sermons.

Symbiotic relations also bleed, because they experience life together.

Simply put, people believe what they do more than do what they believe.

My sermon preparation involves more than commentary study and outlines. I also identify how I can get people talking (go deep and go home). Furthermore, a great message is memorable, and nothing lasts longer on the brain than an experience and a visual tattoo.

So let me bleed for you a little and show you how this works.

For every message, think in three veins:

- **Relationships:** How can I create interactivity?
- **Experiences:** How can I help my hearers feel the message personally?
- **Images:** How can I reinvent this passage/story into a fresh visual metaphor?

In the great Northwest, there's a popular sporting goods and outdoor store known as REI. This chain of stores values experiential shopping. While every outlet offers different amenities, shoppers can rock climb, fly fish, and a whole host of other outdoor activities inside an REI store. REI stands for "recreational equipment incorporated."

It also outlines the three qualities that attract and engage the postmodern mind: **R**elationships, **E**xperiences, and **I**mages. If you can master how to craft interactive, sensory, and visual messages, you'll enjoy success among younger audiences. Throughout this book I've used visual metaphors to help you learn. In the last chapter you discovered the power and purpose of interactivity. It's now time to make it sticky.

Experiences glue everything together. If they can't feel it, they won't live it.

THE HUNT IS ON

Few things score the mind like hunting. I grew up in Montana and lived in a house that ate, drank, and breathed hunting. I shot my first buck when I was 12 years old. I can still tell you what was playing on the radio that morning ("Forever in Blue Jeans" by Neil Diamond), where we were exactly on that mountain road, and even the smell of my grandfather's aftershave. I can recall just like it was yesterday every detail of my finding, sighting, and shooting that buck.

I also vividly remember the last buck I ever shot.

It was a cold late November day. The mountain ground was covered with crunchy 6-inch deep snow, and temperatures were dipping into single digits. My brother and I were hunkered down in a haystack trying to keep warm while my grandfather worked the trees to push out the deer. It was the last day of the season my senior year of high school. The sun was starting to set, and time was running out.

I glassed (surveyed with binoculars) a small meadow to my right when I saw the 5X5 white-tail buck amble into the clearing with a couple does. I watched it for several minutes, less than 100 yards away, and then put my gun site on its chest. With a slow squeeze of the trigger, a boom that echoed for miles and wisp of gunpowder smoke in the air, I watched the buck drop with a perfect shot.

I could see my breath and felt the deep chill of mountain air soak my bones as I approached the buck, now lying lifeless in the snow. I thanked God for giving me a clean shot and the buck for giving me his life. The venison would feed our family throughout the winter months. I then took a knife and began to gut the deer, but in doing so I had to remove my gloves. Instantly the single-digit temperatures hardened my fingers and made the work tedious. All I could think about was getting warm. As I reached inside the carcass to remove the bowels, the still warm blood baptized my hands and thawed them. I relaxed to enjoy the feeling. The steam of the deer against my face was also a blessing.

(I realize for some of my readers, you might find this tale distasteful, even disgusting, but I hope you'll read on.)

It was the blood of that deer that warmed fingers on their way to frostbite. As my numb digits returned to life, I quickly finished the job and pulled my prize buck back to the vehicle. I can still feel my fingers inside that deer. In many ways I was never more alive than in that single moment.

It's an experience that has tattooed my life with a story worth telling (even if it was a bit bloody).

Preaching that communicates will be like hot blood on cold hearts. We live in a frozen culture, iced over by evil and cold in the pain. We all come to church frostbitten and looking for warmth. Jesus told Thomas that all he needed to do was put his hands inside the wounds (John 20:27) to experience the reality of his resurrection. Similarly, our messages must bleed warm blood and invite our hearers to reach inside this ancient yet living Jewish Messiah and sense the cleansing power only he brings.

Experience is a tremendous tutor.

And it's the secret to getting our messages underneath the skin. Remember that Band-Aids are good applications, but they fall off in time. The only way to permanently ink a person's life is by tattoo. Go deep and go home. And every tattoo is rooted in personal experience.

So how do we do it?

Simple. We HUNT. It's a four-part process that guarantees a person doesn't walk away without blood on their hands and feeling warmed by faith, hope, and love. Of course, it starts by getting outdoors. You can't hunt inside a box and neither can your listeners. So to help you understand the process, I'm going to create a message: one topical (life's pressures) and the other more theological (incarnation of Jesus).

HUNT-ING

The glue that makes Scriptures stick long-term is experience. The more we can get our listeners to feel our messages—through their five senses—the better they will stick. So let me get practical. Once I have my study of the Scripture or topic finished, I start every sermon with a simple declarative statement:

Life's problems and pain can be overcome through Jesus.

God revealed his love for mankind by becoming human.

The next step is to decide on a visual metaphor to hook my listeners and create an "eye-dea" for the listener's memory. Sometimes I might use an overarching visual metaphor for a whole series. For example, I have several messages from Philippians that I've wrapped under a "journey" theme (a perfect summer study). One sermon used the Appalachian Trail as the metaphor (our town was on the trail). Another sermon blended the primary points into classic rock songs to create a "road tune" playlist. Still another used motorcycles.

Life's pressures: a traffic jam

Incarnation: a player-coach

Jesus was a master communicator who used experiences as teachable moments. Luke records a particular episode that happened just after Christ's crucifixion about two depressed disciples:

Now that same day two of them were going to a village called Emmaus, about seven miles from Jerusalem. They were talking with each other about everything that had happened. As they talked and discussed these things with each other, Jesus himself came up and walked along with them; but they were kept from recognizing him. (Luke 24:13-16)

We can draw several conclusions from this opening scene:

- Any place and any time can become a "Jesus moment."
- People enter "Jesus moments" in conversation about their life.
- Jesus initiates contact by presence.
- Initially Jesus is unrecognizable.

Every message needs to incarnate into the lives of the listeners. It's not about you but them. What do they need? What do you hear them talking about? Initially, the eyes are blinded to the Presence, but don't stop walking with them.

H: HARVEST AN EMOTION

Now it's time to create a feeling. This is what Jesus did best. He always left his audiences emotionally disturbed. Jesus routinely generated feelings of sadness (rich young ruler), madness (Pharisees and Sadducees), and gladness (Zachaeus). Each of these emotions started through a personal experience with Jesus. In the story of the Emmaus disciples, Jesus harvests an emotion of deep sadness. Ironically, he doesn't preach to them. Instead he listens. He lets them tell their version of the story (Luke 24:19-24).

A bloody sermon doesn't start with an instruction. It begins with inspection.

We need to harvest an emotion.

> "He asked them, 'What are you discussing together as you walk along?' **They stood still, their faces downcast.**"
>
> —Luke 24:17

If my visual metaphor is a "traffic jam," I might ask: What does a traffic jam feel like? For incarnation I might ask: What would incarnation look, sound, and feel like? This is a crucial moment. Your ability to create a feeling that can be explored, applied, and processed through a biblical lens is critical. Here are a few experiences I've done in various sermons over the years to create an emotion:

- Hand folding (opposite thumb on top): Feelings generated include distaste, painful, odd, wrong.
- Hold arms straight out: Feelings generated include pain, giving up.
- Bang a drum every 5 minutes: Feelings of sudden awareness.
- Stand on one leg: Feelings generated include pain, awkwardness, inability.
- Blindfold/close eyes: Feelings produced include lostness, fear, loneliness.
- Marble in shoe: Feelings generated include pain, discomfort.
- Suck on something sweet, bitter, or sour: Feelings created range from pleasure to distaste to dislike.

For a message on life's pressures, I could have the audience stand and form a circle group of six to eight people. The group selects a leader, who places his or her hand in the middle. Then half the group places their hands on top of the leader's (to push down), while the other half places their hands beneath the leader's (to push up). On "go!" the leader would definitely feel pressure (good and bad!). The goal: Create an emotion and/or feeling for what pressure feels like in our lives.

For a message on the Incarnation, I want my hearers to feel how distant God is and how close Christ can become. Perhaps I would open the message speaking backstage or from the back of the room or the balcony. All people would hear is a voice. I could share for several minutes how the ancients believed the gods lived far away from humans. When I start to speak of Jesus and his incarnation, I could appear. I could walk from the back to the front or from the balcony to the stage. I could preach from the floor, up close and personal, touching listeners appropriately through a handshake, fist bump, or pat on the shoulder.

The power of an experience is how many senses the listener uses. I believe in the power of three. Sight. Sound. Touch. If I can fold in taste and smell, that's even better. But here's the kicker: I don't create an experience for experience-sake. It must be processed through conversation and debriefing to be effective:

Life's pressures: How did it feel to be caught in the middle (for the leader)? Was it easier to push down or up? Why? How is this experience like or unlike the pressures we feel daily in our lives?

Incarnation: How did you feel when you finally could see the preacher? How did you feel as he revealed himself to you, perhaps even touched you? How is this experience like or unlike how God incarnated himself to become a human?

Ultimately, you want to harvest an emotion. It's not enough to create one; you need to be able to observe your audience truly feeling the emotion. If they don't feel it, then the experience was just a missed shot.

U: UNCOVER AN INTERPRETATION

Once an emotion is harvested, the next step is to uncover an interpretation. Jesus learned very quickly from the Emmaus disciples that their sadness was rooted in disappointment. Even though they had heard rumors Jesus was alive, they didn't believe it. They wanted to believe it, but it seemed too fantastic an idea. All they knew was the body was missing and some women claimed he was alive.

> "But **we had hoped** that he was the one who was going to redeem Israel."
>
> —Luke 24:21

We all interpret our experiences through how we feel. This past weekend I traveled to a distant city to enjoy a meal with a friend. We picked out a restaurant online and met there. The Internet reviews were amazing for this off-the-beaten-path Italian restaurant, but when I opened the door and walked inside, the décor and plain furnishings surprised me. I felt cheated and slightly angry. It was nothing like I expected. I was disappointed.

Consequently, I interpreted the experience poorly. We ordered very little and found a different place in town for a meal. What we ate was good but nothing spectacular, and I doubt I'll return there anytime soon.

This is the problem with most preaching.

Our listeners already arrive loaded heavily with emotional baggage. And if we're not careful we can spin further negative emotions (boredom, apathy, anger, unworthiness) in our hearers. Every feeling (good, bad, or otherwise) is interpreted and applied. That's why master communicators always speak to the heart first and create positive emotions like pleasure, insightfulness, usefulness, and positivity.

Once an experience has created an emotion, make sure you don't move on without uncovering an interpretation, because if you don't, the audience will.

Life's pressures: In the pressure of the experience, we still have a choice to live up or down.

Incarnation: The uniqueness of Christianity is a present and personal God.

N: NOURISH A BELIEF

Jesus knew the Emmaus disciples had misinterpreted their feelings. Sadness was acceptable, but evidently they had forgotten not only what the Scriptures taught (through Moses and the prophets) but also what he had taught them personally.

This is where a little sermonizing is a good thing. But I suspect Jesus used interaction and dialogue as his strategy far more than a roadside lecture. Regardless of how Jesus did it, Luke clearly reveals that he explained "what was said in all the Scriptures concerning himself" (Luke 24:27). Sometimes we need to nourish a belief.

> "He said to them, 'How foolish you are, and how slow to believe all that the prophets have spoken! Did not the Messiah have to suffer these things and then enter his glory?' And beginning with Moses and all the Prophets, he explained to them what was said in all the Scriptures concerning himself."
> —Luke 24:25-27

Of course, this is where every experience is different and can create a host of possible beliefs. The emotions created from the experience produce an interpretation (positive, negative, neutral) that inspires a belief. If our listeners arrive hungry but leave bored, apathetic, or unworthy (interpreting the feelings this way), it's not hard to understand how they'll eventually believe church is a boring place, Christianity is ho-hum, and they are spiritually unworthy.

Conversation is the key.

No experience, or the emotion it creates, should be an island.

Rather, it's important to nourish a belief through targeted questions that get to the heart and the head.

Life's pressures: When you reflect on the hand experience, what pressures do you currently face? What is pushing you down in life? Or holding you up? What kind of person are you in your relationships? Do you build others up and encourage or push people down through discouragement? In your heart of hearts, what kind of person do you want to be for others? Why?

Incarnation: When you reflect on how you felt during the incarnation experience, how close do you feel to God right now? Do you feel Jesus is side-stage, back row, or out of sight? Why? When is God closer than you think? How can you be like Jesus and draw near to someone hurting, helpless, or hopeless?

If you nourish a belief that helps people get beyond the baggage they hauled into the message experience, it's a win. Sometimes the insight is small and predictable, but sometimes the light bulb pops on and big changes are on the horizon. When we create attractional experiences that spark new values, understanding, and beliefs, people won't want it to end.

When's the last time you had that happen when you preached?

The Emmaus disciples were so enthralled by Jesus (even though they still didn't recognize him as Jesus) that they "urged him strongly" to stay the night at their place (Luke 24:29). Master communicators create environments that produce raucous affection, radical adoration, and rabid allegiance. People won't want to go home.

T: TRAIN A BEHAVIOR

Ultimately, every message must target a specific behavior. If our preaching doesn't change lives, then we aren't preaching.

For the Emmaus disciples, they invited Jesus in for the night and dined with him around a rather common table. And yet, in that equally ordinary moment, the extraordinary happened. As Jesus blessed and broke the bread, "Their eyes were opened and they recognized him" (verse 31). In a moment, Jesus was real. In just a split second, Jesus became relevant. This man was no mere mortal: He was Messiah.

But don't miss what happened next.

Luke records that Jesus vanishes and these two formerly distraught disciples return immediately to Jerusalem to tell the other disciples. They ventured back during the night when roads were most dangerous. In fact, no sane ancient person traveled at night. Convenience and comfort were not an issue for these two disciples. They had experienced Jesus personally. It was do or die, and either way was a win.

A sermon without life change is like a car without gas. It's nice to look at. It might even have some function as a resting place, but it doesn't go anywhere.

Every message needs to target specific life changes. What do you want your listeners to do specifically?

> **They got up and returned at once to Jerusalem.** There they found the Eleven and those with them, assembled together and saying, 'It is true! The Lord has risen and has appeared to Simon.'"
>
> —Luke 24:33-34

Life's pressures: In the coming week, identify a single strategy you can employ to help you overcome life's pressures…then practice it daily.

Incarnation: In the next seven days, operate like Jesus might in your world. WWJD. What would Jesus do? Write your experiences in a journal.

After all, Jesus might be waiting on us to act before he can. It's interesting that Jesus appears to these two Emmaus disciples, who then hurry back to Jerusalem to tell the eleven disciples. But Jesus doesn't appear to these other disciples until they do (Luke 24:36).

Sometimes God is waiting on us to act before he can use us fully.

Blood is life.

When it becomes diseased or disabled, when it ceases to course through a human's arteries, death is imminent. The heart is what pumps the blood. Life happens only because the heart does its job.

It's time you and I did our job. We are the cardiac communicators. If we fail to beat, pump, and push the blood through the body of Christ, it becomes a deathwatch. Jesus is the head, and the Holy Spirit lives inside the heart. The Holy Spirit lives within us. Our divine role and eternal responsibility is to ensure the blood flows strong, free, and rich.

Biologically, the oxygen-rich blood flows through the arteries into the farthest reaches of a human's flesh. As the blood feeds the body, it returns to the heart via veins to re-oxygenate. This natural cycle happens countless times every day. We don't even think about it. Blood flows. Flesh feeds. Veins carry. The heart pumps. The lungs contribute.

At no point can the heart rest.

And neither can we.

Every Sunday, our listeners arrive to get to the heart of the matter. Our homilies re-oxygenate tired souls and pump them back into their secular worlds to be the light and salt and water. Consequently, our relationship with our hearers is symbiotic. They need us. We need them. God needs us.

We are his blood to a world hungry for transfusion and transformation.

John Phipps scrawled "I love my kids" in his own blood. Jesus did the same thing on a cross 2,000 years ago.

Every Sunday and in every message, we need to bleed similar words:

> "I love Jesus."
>
> > "I love his church."
> >
> > > "I love the Kingdom."

Endnotes

1. Marla Lehner, "Train Wreck Survivor Pens Love Note in Blood," *People Magazine*, February 4, 2005, http://www.people.com/people/article/0,,1024872,00.html.

2. Leonard Sweet, *Giving Blood: A Fresh Paradigm for Preaching* (Grand Rapids, MI: Zondervan, 2014), 25.

3. John 19:34: "Instead, one of the soldiers pierced Jesus' side with a spear, bringing a sudden flow of blood and water."

4. Hebrews 9:18-20: "This is why even the first covenant was not put into effect without blood. When Moses had proclaimed every command of the law to all the people, he took the blood of calves, together with water, scarlet wool and branches of hyssop, and sprinkled the scroll and all the people. He said, 'This is the blood of the covenant, which God has commanded you to keep.'"

5. Hebrews 9:14-15: "How much more, then, will the blood of Christ, who through the eternal Spirit offered himself unblemished to God, cleanse our consciences from acts that lead to death, so that we may serve the living God! For this reason Christ is the mediator of a new covenant, that those who are called may receive the promised eternal inheritance—now that he has died as a ransom to set them free from the sins committed under the first covenant."

6. John describes the Great Prostitute Babylon in Revelation 17:6: "I saw that the woman was drunk with the blood of God's holy people, the blood of those who bore testimony to Jesus."

7. Luke 22:20: "In the same way, after the supper he took the cup, saying, 'This cup is the new covenant in my blood, which is poured out for you.'"

8. Hebrews 9:22: "In fact, the law requires that nearly everything be cleansed with blood, and without the shedding of blood there is no forgiveness."

9. Acts 1:18-19: "With the payment he received for his wickedness, Judas bought a field; there he fell headlong, his body burst open and all his intestines spilled out. Everyone in Jerusalem heard about this, so they called that field in their language Akeldama, that is, Field of Blood."

10. Revelation 19:13: "He is dressed in a robe dipped in blood, and his name is the Word of God."

11. Leonard Sweet, *Giving Blood: A Fresh Paradigm for Preaching* (Grand Rapids, MI: Zondervan, 2014), 22.

AFTERWORD

Change never comes easy.

Just ask the Swedes.

For most of the 20th century they had driven on the left side of the road. It was how they learned to drive, what they liked, and it was a cultural transportation tradition. Nevertheless, there was growing alarm over accidents and fatalities on Swedish roads. Too many people were getting hurt or killed. Many experts believed it was because Swedes mostly drove cars with a left-side steering wheel (on the left side of the road). Consequently, head-on crashes and car-pedestrian accidents were common, and transportation officials were concerned.

Sweden neighbored countries—Finland and Norway—that already drove on the right side of the road, so switching wasn't without precedent. Still, for four decades the Swedes overwhelmingly voted down referendum after referendum to switch lanes. Finally, in 1963 a vote passed that initiated a four-year transition to move Swedes from driving on the left side to the right side of the road.

The change was called "H Day," or "Högertrafikomläggningen," for "The right-hand traffic diversion," and it was slated for Sunday, September 3, 1967. For years, Swedish psychologists monitored the transition. Jingles were crafted and sung to promote the change. Even commemorative stuff was sold to mark the special day. "H Day" was one very special Swedish day.

The day of the big switch was a fascinating study in how to change. With precise planning H Day successfully engineered a totally new way to drive in Sweden. At precisely 4:50 a.m. all traffic came to a complete stop and then switched lanes like a national syncopated traffic troupe. At 5 a.m. it was official. Swedes now drove on the right side of the road.

Dozens of years of resistance. Four years of preparation. Ten minutes of transition.

Somehow I don't think the church will change with as much unity. We can only agree to be disagreeable. When tradition hardens into traditionalism there's a problem. Tradition is the living faith of the dead. Traditionalism is the dead faith of the living. Most Protestant churches and denominations view change like some Americans see guns: You'll have to pry it from my dead fingers.

I've got news for you: The postmodern generations prefer driving on the right side, and as long as the church remains locked inside formats—particularly a 30 to 50 minute lecture on Sunday morning—it will be out of touch. The modern homily is an academic exercise. It's time for our own "H Day." Can you HEAR me now? Few (under 50) are listening anymore.

The problem is most established U.S. churches won't come to their senses soon enough. I have no doubt that by the end of the 21st century the format for church will reflect a more Web-wired visual world. Our systems will be interactive, experiential, and image-soaked. I have no doubt the sermon, as one-way communication, will be history. In fact, our grandchildren will probably be amazed that we once went to church and listened to a preacher talk for almost an hour.

I also have no doubt that Christianity will survive and thrive in this wet, Web world, but it's not going to happen easily. We will get wet on this ride. And we'll have to switch lanes to do it.

Just yesterday a megachurch worship pastor asked me about how to convert their 2000-member congregation worship service into an interactive, experiential, visual "hot spot." I told him to forget it. The ship had already sailed for his church. All he had to do was look around at the faces: wrinkled, gray, and bald. The average age of this dynamic congregation of senior saints is 55.

I told him to undergo a change so radical would burst the wineskin.

In reality, I only see three types of churches who can convert to conversational, experiential, and image-driven preaching.

THE SMALLER CHURCH

It's easier to turn around a Toyota in a traffic jam than a tractor-trailer.

The smaller church is uniquely wired in a postmodern culture to change faster and with more fluidity. The large and megachurch congregations will struggle and suffer due to their organizational bulk. Small is tall in a Starbucks culture. In fact, the micro-church (or house church) is the perfect laboratory for interactive, experiential, and visually stimulated preaching. The living room is a far better hot spot for faith conversations. The smaller church has a decided edge.

THE NEW CHURCH

A second church with an advantage is the church plant.

A church, like any living organism or organization, has a developmental point where its DNA hardens. Most believe this setting happens sometime before a church's 10th birthday. It's at this point that a congregation is hardened around certain undeniable and unequivocal values. Consequently, the time to initiate a big switch in preaching format is when the cement is still fresh and moldable. If you wait too long, the wineskin turns rigid and brittle.

THE DYING CHURCH WITH STAINED-GLASSED STEEPLED PROPERTY

Surprisingly, a final church with hope to make the switch is a congregation on life support. However, there is a caveat: A young pastor and leadership must lead the transition. Older pastors (over 50) will balk at these changes naturally. It takes far too much energy and most simply can't conceive the change.

But if you're in a church that has a steeple and stained glass, count yourself fortunate. Postmoderns love to congregate in these spiritual spaces.

Recently I helped a Generation X pastor in a small Oregon town reimagine his church. He had read the cultural tea leaves and agreed the postmodern generations weren't coming to church anymore. His church building is a gorgeous steepled property with much potential. In a brainstorming session he reimagined his church as a cultural learning center, a community-gathering place, and even a restaurant/ coffee shop. He confessed his church building wasn't obsolete, but his Sunday morning preaching strategy certainly was!

The good news about Christianity is it's all about resurrections.

The majority of U.S. congregations will simply wake up one day and smell the proverbial coffee…emanating from countless new churches that reinvented their Sunday mornings into an interactive, visual experience. Most will no doubt do what all churches do in a crisis, and that's beg, borrow, and steal what has worked elsewhere, but it'll be too late. The ship will have sailed. Those who try to pour new Jesus-java into old modern wineskins will only fissure not fix the problem.

I know this news won't be welcome in a lot of churches or even ministry training schools still stuck in 1995. But ignoring the problem will only make it worse, so if you have no intention or desire to reach and teach the postmodern generations (born since 1960) then I encourage you to keep driving on the left side for as long and as far as you can.

Just know that one day you'll suddenly figure out the lanes have switched and you're now headed in the wrong direction.

Overall, I remain wildly confident the church's best days still lie ahead. But only if we recommit to an Acts 2:42 format that revolves around four key elements: the apostle's doctrine, fellowship, breaking of bread (Lord's Supper), and prayer. To be culturally relevant, we'll have to initiate these four elements through conversation, experience, and image.

We'll have to think small. We'll have go deep. We'll have to preach different.

Ultimately, we'll have to change lanes. And learn to drive on the right side.

Change happens. Change has happened. Change *will* happen.

Endnote

1. The Beatles, "Eleanor Rigby," *Revolver* (album), 1966.

ACKNOWLEDGEMENTS

Writing a book is like giving birth to an elephant.

From conception to birth, it takes nearly two years of hard labor, deep thought, and many midwives. And so a few back slaps and thank yous are definitely in order for the arrival of this "baby":

- I'm thankful for Thom and Joani Schultz, Chris Yount-Jones, and all my friends at Group Publishing for taking a chance on this title. I'm especially grateful to Amy Nappa, my pitch person, for her faith in this project and my editor, Bob D'Ambrosio, for his skill in focusing my thoughts and correcting my grammar.

- I also want to thank a few churches that allowed me the opportunity to explore my emerging ideas on preaching in the 21st century: Cornerstone Christian Church (Duncannon, Pennsylvania), Foothills Christian Church (Boise, Idaho), and Athena Christian Church (Athena, Oregon).

- Much of this book found its genesis in my preaching courses at Northwest University (Southern Idaho campus) in Nampa, Idaho. So here's to these students for framing my thoughts: Keil Alloway, Hubert Anika, Rojelio Aquila, Dan and Sylvia Hendricks, Rachel and Ken Maxwell, Michael McCormick, Katie Roberts, Clay Ramirez, Kay Rhoads, Jose Ruano, Pavel Shulga, Marvin Smith, Isaac Tellez, and Jesse Trujillo. Also a special shout out to John Wilkie for hiring me to teach at the site.

- A special nod to the man who (thankfully) ruined my life for Jesus and the Kingdom: Leonard Sweet. I'm not only proud to be one of his students but also his friend and colleague.

- Dr. Richard Brown, my preaching professor at Nebraska Christian College. He taught me how to preach and how to love the church. Thanks Doc!

- I also want to recognize a wide variety of individuals (most living and some famous) who inspired my insights and practices for preaching in the church (in no particular order): Delbert Durfee, Jason Carman, Matt Sutman, Mike Maglish, Mister Rogers, Nathan Wyatt, Rick Page, Steve Moore, Ronald Reagan, Steve Crane, Ryan Chromey, Derek Voorhees, Ben McClary, Phil, Willie and Jase Robertson, Dennis McManamon, Mehmet Oz, Sara Jane Weidner, Keith Green, Allen Wolves, Jeff Walling, Ken Burns, Steve McConkey, Jeff Probst, David Fincher, Ben Bauman, Scott Riggin, David Roadcup, Michael Scott, Scot Longyear, Martin Luther King,

David Christensen, Carl Holmes, Rich Mullins, Brad Henson, David Rumpke, Titus Benton, Robin Sigars, Doug and Tamy Lay, Justin Sturgeon, Steve Taylor, Tim Nischan, Randy Bourn, Justin Herman, Matt Proctor, Sharon McDowell, David McDonald, Justin Foster, Chuck Conniry, Dean and Lisa Sakamoto, Garth Brooks, Mark Moore, Vincent Kituku, Tim and Karen Alberts, Joseph Myers, Rich Knopp, Stephen Campbell, Mark Maddix, Lucas Rouggly, David Mehrle, Russell Clum, Keith Wilson, Bonnie Morrison, Shan Moyers, Eddie Rester, Alan Ehler, Mike Breaux, Steve Jobs, Cal Jernigan, Michelle Asous, Mark Krause, Chris Renzelman, Aaron Chambers, Johnny Cash, Mike Yaconelli, Les Christie, Johnathan Mast, Ron and Lois McConkey, John Tietsort, Don Raymond, Tim Nay, Greg Baird, Jim Putman, Chris Kelly, Dan Kimball, and Brian Jones.

⁕ To anyone I might have missed, this line is for you. Thanks.

Appendix One
20 RESOURCES FOR PREACHING IN A FLUID CULTURE

VISUAL RESOURCES:

1. **PowToons**: powtoons.com
   Create short cartoons to illustrate points.

2. **Videoblocks**: videoblocks.com
   Thousands of short videos to illustrate.

3. **Wingclips**: wingclips.com
   Spice up your sermon with a movie clip.

4. **Graceway Media**: gracewaymedia.com
   Stills, motions, and countdowns.

5. **Share Faith**: sharefaith.com
   All-in-one place for visual media.

6. **Worship House Media**: worshiphousemedia.com
   My favorite place to visually illustrate all my messages!

7. **Free Worship Backgrounds**: worshipbackgroundsforfree.com
   Find countdowns, worship backgrounds, and more.

8. **Church Visuals**: churchvisuals.com
   Lots of freebies!

INTERACTIVE AND EXPERIENTIAL RESOURCES/HELPS:

9. **God Space: Where Spiritual Conversations Happen Naturally**
   by Doug Pollock (Group)

10. **R.E.A.L.: Surprisingly Simple Ways to Engage Adults** (Group)

11. **Why Nobody Wants to Be Around Christians Anymore**
by Thom and Joani Schultz (Group)

12. **Serendipity Bible** (Zondervan)
Every passage is connected to "open," "study," and "application" questions.
Hands down the best (and only) Bible small group leaders will ever need.

13. **Lifetree Café**: lifetreecafe.com
A resource that provides an interactive, experiential, visual faith community.

14. **How To Ask Great Questions**
by Karen Lee-Thorp (NavPress)

15. **Nothing Never Happens: Experiential Learning**
by John D. Hendrix (Smyth & Helwys Publishing)

PRESENTATION RESOURCES:

16. **Prezi**: prezi.com
Make your presentations flow and move like never before.

17. **Keynote Theme Park**: keynotethemepark.com
For Mac and iPad Keynote users!

18. **Simply the Best Fonts**: simplythebest.net/fonts
Great free fonts.

BIBLE STUDY AND COMMENTARY RESOURCES:

19. **Bible Hub**: biblehub.com
A winning combination for biblical study.

20. **Bible Study Tools**: biblestudytools.com
Commentaries and more.

Appendix Two
THE SERMON PROCESS

SELECT A PASSAGE OR TOPIC:

THE MAIN IDEA:
(in 10 words or less)

STEP ONE: STUDY THE PASSAGE

Write a 2,000 word personal commentary. Read at least ten different biblical commentaries/dictionaries/websites on the passage or topic. Study the Greek or Hebrew. Immerse yourself in the culture and context.

DESIGN/DISTRIBUTE COMMENTARY before or after the message.

STEP TWO: FOCUS THE PASSAGE

Write ONE idea/insight you want your people to remember.
(ex. The congregation will discover Paul's definition of love in 1 Corinthians 13.)

Write ONE attitude/value/belief you want your people to feel.
(ex. The congregation will feel the true nature of love.)

Write ONE behavior or life change you'd like your people to do.
(ex. The congregation will engineer "pay it forward" acts of love in the coming week.)

STEP THREE: VISUALIZE THE PASSAGE

Review the passage or topic and develop a VISUAL METAPHOR to serve as a bridge between the Scripture/topic and your audience.

CREATE A VISUAL METAPHOR:

Is it relevant (will your audience connect)?

Is it simple (will your audience understand)?

Is it powerful (will your audience remember)?

Is it personal (will your audience apply it to their life)?

STEP FOUR: EXPERIENCE THE PASSAGE

Review the ATTITUDE/VALUE/BELIEF that you want to explore and, in particular, the FEELING. How can you get your people to FEEL that feeling through an experience?

CREATE AN EXPERIENCE TO HOOK YOUR AUDIENCE:

Does it evoke the desired emotion?

Does it involve everyone in the audience?

Does it include a time to debrief the experience (conversation)?

Is it adventuresome? Does it produce alternative feelings?

STEP FIVE: MEMORIALIZE THE PASSAGE

CREATE AN OUTLINE TO HELP YOUR AUDIENCE REMEMBER:

Remember the rule of threes: we remember things better in threes.

Use a mnemonic device: alliteration, story/parable, acronym.

Use a visual for each main point, movement, or shift.

Choose 2-3 video clips to foster engagement and retention
(using YouTube, Worship House Media, Wingclips, etc.)

Choose 2-3 illustrations, quotes, statistics, or other insights
from your biblical study to explain and apply the passage.

STEP SIX: DIALOGUE THE PASSAGE

CREATE CONVERSATIONS TO HELP YOUR AUDIENCE INTERACT:

Identify at least THREE times when the audience can stop for several minutes to process the information and/or message experience.

AFTER YOUR EXPERIENCE (2-5 minutes)

AFTER YOU'VE INTRODUCED/EXPLAINED THE PASSAGE (5-10 minutes)

AFTER YOU'VE GIVEN A PRIMARY APPLICATION (5-10 minutes)

Hint: Use the Serendipity Bible to help you draft and ask powerful questions. Use pairs, trios, quads, and groups no larger than six. The goal is to allow the audience to interact as much as you will explain/apply passage.

STEP SEVEN: TATTOO THE PASSAGE

CREATE LIFE CHANGE IN YOUR AUDIENCE:

Review the one thing you wanted your audience to change, specifically, or do in the coming week to show the message was tattooed into their life.

Develop a brief closing LIFE CHALLENGE that specifically identifies several choices to live out the Scripture/topic in the coming week. If appropriate, practice the challenge as part of the message and within the sermon time.

Ultimately your goal is to create a MESSAGE EXPERIENCE that your people feel/sense, think deeply about, and can visualize.

The EXPERIENCE needs to be 50/50: Half the time invested in message explanation/ exploration, primary application, and the experience. The other half used to allow the audience to interact with each other through conversation.

Post Message Evaluation

- Did the audience remember your main idea? Why or why not?

- Did the audience feel/sense your message idea? Why or why not?

- Did the audience leave with a strong visual? Why or why not?

• How much time did the audience spend interacting?

• How much time did you spend talking to them?

• What would you do differently if you preached this message again? Why?

• After three days, ask two to four people what they remember about your message.

∘ Was your message creative, empowering, insightful, helpful? Why or why not?

∘ Did you start and end on time? If no, why not?

∘ Did you explore and debrief the experience? If no, why not?

∘ Were your visuals dynamic, engaging, and attractive? If no, why not?

Notes

Notes

Notes